Prepare for Greatness:
How to Make Your Success Inevitable

- by Everett Ofori

© 2013 by Everett Ofori. All rights reserved. No part of this book may be reproduced in any form or by any electronic or mechanical means, including information storage and retrieval systems without the permission in writing from the publisher, except by a reviewer, who may quote brief passages in a review.

Cover design: Raphaël Genty

Author contact:
Everett Ofori
Takarazuka University of Art and Design
Tokyo Campus Bldg. 1F-123MBE
7-11-1 Nishi-Shinjuku, Shinjuku-ku
Tokyo, Japan 160-0023

Email: everettofori@gmail.com

International Standard Book Number
10-digit ISBN: 0-921143-00-1
13-digit ISBN: 978-0-921143-00-0

Canadian Cataloguing in Publication Data
  Ofori, Everett, (Date)
      Prepare for greatness

      Includes bibliographical references and index.
      ISBN 0-921143-00-1
      13-digit ISBN: 978-0-921143-00-0

     1. Success. 2. Goal (Psychology). I.
International Financial Freedom Institute.
II. Title.
BF637.S8034 1993   158'.1   C93-091585-2

> I must admit that I personally measure success in terms of the contributions an individual makes to her or his fellow human beings.
> - Margaret Mead in Redbook (1978)

Dedicated - with love - to Mom,
Ellen Harriet Reynolds,
Who gave me an appreciation for words

And to the memory of Grandma,
Eliza Aba Duncan,
Whose wisdom gives me the courage to persist

> Lives of great men all remind us
> We can make our lives sublime
> And departing, leave behind us
> Footprints on the sands of time
> - Henry Wadsworth Longfellow

Other Books by Everett Ofori

- Succeeding from the Margins of Canadian Society: A Strategic Resource for New Immigrants, Refugees and International Students (with Dr. Francis Adu-Febiri, *Professor of Sociology & Anthropology, Canada*)

- Read Assure: Guaranteed Formula for Reading Success with Phonics

- Guaranteed Formula for Writing Success

- Guaranteed Formula for Public Speaking Success

- The Changing Japanese Woman: From Yamatonadeshiko to YamatonadeGucci

> The heights (to which) great men (and women) reached and kept;
> Were not attained by sudden flight
> But they, while their companions slept
> Were toiling upwards in the night.
>
> - Henry Wadsworth Longfellow

Acknowledgments

This book is hardly the product of a singular effort. I am greatly indebted to all the professionals who responded to my inquiries for the secrets of their success. Thank you.

Gratitude also goes to Aviva Laye who both challenged and inspired me by her commitment to clarity and pursuit of editorial excellence. Thanks also to Heather Conn and Ted Cheney for their invaluable editorial input. Naturally, as the author I take full responsibility for this work.

Some of the contributors to this book have passed away, but their insights and wisdom will nourish other lives for generations to come.

May their souls, therefore, rest in well-deserved peace.

- Everett Ofori

Preface

Throughout history, certain people have distinguished themselves so much in various fields that their names have become synonymous with greatness. In the area of social justice, the names Mahatma Gandhi, Abraham Lincoln, and Martin Luther King Jr. come immediately to mind. Great men like Napoleon, Alexander the Great, and Charlemagne are known for their military exploits. Still others have been hailed as great because of their selfless devotion: Nelson Mandela, for example, for seeking freedom for South Africa's disenfranchised majority, and Mother Teresa, for her work in alleviating the suffering of the poor in the slums of India.

PREPARE FOR GREATNESS: HOW TO MAKE YOUR SUCCESS INEVITABLE emphasizes the value of preparation as imperative to the success of any undertaking. There is an abundance of both historical and contemporary examples of "preparation for greatness" and yet, somehow we repeatedly fail to take the kinds of actions that will move us relentlessly toward our own goals. We fail to discover the kinds of skills, either personal or technical, that we need to master in order to achieve our goals.

Fortunately, not everyone wants to conquer nations and not everyone wants to influence a whole nation. But, many a person has arrived at the twilight of life only to fall to grief over missed opportunities, for not having pursued a dream. He realizes too late that he has been carried through life on a raft, beaten about by the prevailing currents over which he has exerted no influence.

Yes, *Prepare for Greatness* and make your success inevitable. Greatness for a single parent may be the ability to provide sustenance for the family. Greatness for a newly married man may be his ability to satisfy the whims and caprices of his darling wife. To a university freshman, greatness may be overcoming the challenge to earn a degree that may be the ticket to success in the real world.

Each new generation of achievers has its own "prophet" who emphasizes one particular point for the benefit of readers: Dale Carnegie, with *How to Win Friends and Influence People*, W. Clement Stone with *Positive Thinking*, and Tony Robbins with his *Unlimited Power* message. *Prepare for Greatness* is about preparing to win in the game of life, preparing to master life in spite of its petty tyrannies and roadblocks.

Preparation here does not merely signify the acquisition of knowledge or a specific attitude but is far more encompassing. This book highlights preparation as the cornerstone of achievement and touches on qualities which when cultivated and put to use will inevitably contribute to success. This book gives both contemporary and historical examples of people who have applied the principles of determination, commitment and persistence to attain their own greatness. It also includes brief accounts from highly successful people including geneticist David Suzuki, broadcaster Johnny Esaw, entrepreneur Richard Branson, university chancellor Eleanor J. Smith, former Canadian politician Iona Campagnola and Nobel Prize winner Dr. Norman E. Borlaug, who share with readers how the application of certain principles transformed their lives to give them a winning edge.

> **I do not want to die...until I have faithfully made the most of my talent and cultivated the seed that was placed in me until the last small twig has grown.**
> - Kathe Kollwitz in *The Diaries and Letters of Kathe Kollwitz* (1955)

Introduction
- by Joanna Kafarowski

Reading a book that sets your pulse racing and gets the adrenalin pumping surely rates amongst one of life's greatest pleasures. When that book inspires you to action and spurs you on to accomplish great deeds, then it's worth its weight in gold. *Prepare for Greatness* is such a book.

All of us grow to maturity with limitless visions, aspiring to become a world traveller, best-selling author, daring astronaut or wealthy entrepreneur. For most, reality sets in and these idealistic visions dull to be replaced by the need for economic security, the demands of family life and the pressures of a complex world. But dreams never die and *Prepare for Greatness* resuscitates your long-hidden passion and rekindles the desire to realize that goal.

Don't expect this to be an easy book. You won't learn how to become a millionaire in ten quick lessons but how you can reasonably accomplish your goals, whatever they may be. Ever feel you're locked out of a profession because you lack suitable training or because you just don't have the experience? No matter how limited your education, how old you are or how complicated your life situation, if you've got the will, this book will show you the way. Author Everett Ofori shows you how motivation, self-discipline and persistence are the most significant qualities in attaining success. Learn how to harness your personal traits and turn your faults around so they become advantages.

Are you ready for success or do you still harbour doubts about your own abilities? *Prepare for Greatness* helps you confront your fears and discover the talent needed for the future you desire.

Prepare for Greatness by Everett Ofori is a self-help book *par excellence* offering practical advice on how you can make it but it's much more than that. *Prepare for Greatness* is that wise and trusted friend who is constantly at hand, bolstering your ego and leading you down the road to success. So, read on and when you're finished, ask yourself, what's holding me back from fulfilling my dreams?

TABLE OF CONTENTS   Page

Acknowledgments 5
Preface 6
Introduction - by Joanna Kafarowski 8

CHAPTER ONE 15
SELF-EXAMINATION - An Essential First Step
* What's your blueprint for success? - Time is your ally - Does the pursuit of happiness pay? - Clarify your dreams - Write down your goals and follow through - Know thy talent - Be a Master of your dreams - Say to yourself, "I can and I will" - Who needs an education? - Imitate the best; emulate the great - Learn the magic of commitment - Be willing to pay the price of success - THE PREPARATION GAME - PERSONAL PLEDGE - POINTS TO PONDER - SUCCESS TIPS: **Richard McCormick**, CEO, U.S. West Inc., Englewood, Colorado, U.S.A..

CHAPTER TWO 29
CONFRONT YOUR FEARS
* Prepare to conquer fear - Banish your fear of failure; clear the way for success - Pursue excellence, not perfection - Let courage rule - Meet **Sandra Kurtzig** - MANMAN'S Girl - Take action now! - Find the powerful antidote to fear - Take a cue from **Howard Thurston**, showman extraordinaire - TIPS FOR BOOSTING COURAGE - EXERCISE FOR BOOSTING COURAGE - Say "I will" to your dreams

CHAPTER THREE 38
MAKE PERSISTENCE YOUR FRIEND
***Maxcy Filer**, attorney-at-law learns a lesson from persistence - Never give up - Great men and women do know great pains - DON'T QUIT - Don't lose sight of your destination - LESSONS FROM PERSISTENCE - "EXERCISE - ON PERSISTENCE" - The Dominican University Goals Study - SUCCESS TIPS: **Alex Trotman,** chairman and CEO of Ford Motor Company, Dearborn, Michigan, U.S.A.; **Madeleine Stern**, proprietor of Rare Books, New York, N.Y., U.S.A.; **Jacki Sorensen**, aerobic dance company executive, choreographer; Jacki's Inc., Deland, Florida, U.S.A.

CHAPTER FOUR 49
REDISCOVER YOUR TALENTS
* What do you do best? - Allow your talents to lead you - Abraham Lincoln had a winning way with words - Immerse yourself in the milieu of your given talent - Be aware of your options - MOOCs to the rescue - Sit in one chair - Do something well - Enrico Caruso believed in his talent - MAKE THE MOST OF YOUR TALENTS

CHAPTER FIVE 60
DRIVE AND SELF-DISCIPLINE
* You've got to act to achieve - Whatever you can do or dream you can, begin it - If you think you have problems, learn from Helen Keller - Regulate your time - **Josh Weston**'s Rule: "39 + 1 > 40 + 0" - *You* make things happen - Be flexible - Don't blame your failures on a witch - You can benefit from associating with a professional organization - "DRIVE AND DISCIPLINE - IN A NUTSHELL" - SELF-DISCIPLINE THROUGH TIME MANAGEMENT - Discover the role of self-esteem

CHAPTER SIX 70
STRONG EGO
* You need supreme faith - Your unique perspective - "Georgette Mosbacher - Tap into the force within" - Be Yourself or Refashion Yourself? - It's okay to get help - Can ego boosters rescue you? - It's okay to be content - Leave perfection to the heavens - NURTURE YOUR EGO - EGO CHECK - SUCCESS TIPS: **Marjorie Holmes**, author, columnist; Lake Jackson Hills, Manassas, Virginia, U.S.A.

CHAPTER SEVEN 83
EDUCATE YOURSELF TO YOUR OPTIONS IN LIFE
* Pursue knowledge - **Malcolm X:** The transforming power of the word - Profit from the power of knowledge - Gandhi, Nkrumah and L'Amour - You have time, no? - "Read a minimum of one hundred and fifty pages a day," says **Menachem Begin** - Communicate effectively; be a leader - "Public speaking - are you prepared?" - Learning from interviews - An actor prepares; **Anthony Hopkins**' secret - **Matt Damon & Ben Affleck:** Actor/Writer friends - But...What 10,000 hours? - EDUCATE YOURSELF! - Knowledge Quest - SUCCESS TIPS: **John C. Polanyi,** Nobel Prize winner, professor, Department of Chemistry, University of Toronto, Ontario, Canada; **Kazuyoshi Ikeda,** D.Sc., physicist and poet, Osaka, Japan; **Dr. John Howard Gibbons,** government official, physicist, Director of the White House Office of Science and Technology Policy, Washington, D.C., U.S.A.

CHAPTER EIGHT 102
VISUALIZE - AS YOU SEE IT SO IT SHALL BE
* Better a thinking pauper than a prince with half a brain - Power of visualization - Aim for nothing but the best - Fill in knowledge gaps - Short, medium, and long-term goals - "**Lillian Vernon** - A Vision of unparalleled success" - "THE ENTREPRENEUR AND THE PROFESSIONAL MANAGER - GETTING THE BEST OF BOTH WORLDS (by Lillian Vernon)" - Prepare to Pivot - Tell a few good friends - Your friends: Do they have an Identity of Integrity? - POINTS TO PONDER - DAILY VISUALIZATION PRACTICE

CHAPTER NINE 116
TAP INTO THE MENTAL
RESOURCES OF A MENTOR
* Be selective - Make daily resolutions - POINTS FOR REFLECTION - THE ROLE MODEL PROGRAM - SUCCESS TIPS: **Liz Ashton,** president of Camosun College, Victoria, B.C., Canada; **Dr. Shirley A.R. Lewis,** president of Paine College, Augusta, Georgia, U.S.A.; **Dr. Joyce Brothers,** television personality, psychologist, Fort Lee, New Jersey, U.S.A.

CHAPTER TEN 126
COMMITMENT CAN MAKE ALL THE DIFFERENCE
* "**Dr. Beatrice Engstrand** - A Study in Commitment; A Triumph of Determination" - **Nelson Mandela** knows the meaning of commitment - **Mark McCormack** committed himself to quality - **Bill Cosby's** commitment to a dream was two Volkswagens and a $39,000 home - Make time for practice - If you go it alone you have a long way to go - Preparation yields multiple benefits - THE FINAL COMMITMENT

CHAPTER ELEVEN 138
ARE YOU WILLING TO
PAY THE PRICE AND SACRIFICE?
* Where there is a will - Mother Teresa spread compassion - Background of the saint - Three African Nobel laureates:
1) Professor **Wangari Maathai** (*Mottainai*)
2) **Leymah Gbowee:** Tapping into the power within
3) **Ellen Johnson Sirleaf:** Africa's first female president

EXERCISE ON YOUR WILLINGNESS TO SACRIFICE -
Take action and prepare for greatness!

CHAPTER TWELVE 146
MORE TIPS FROM SUCCESSFUL PEOPLE:
Betty M. Wilson - Vice-president, Taxes; and Assistant Secretary, ITT Financial Corporation, St. Louis, Missouri, U.S.A..
Marcel Barbeau - Painter and sculptor, Montreal, Quebec, Canada.
Lillian Vernon - Founder of the Lillian Vernon Corporation, New Rochelle, N.Y., U.S.A.
David Suzuki - Geneticist, broadcaster, lecturer, author, and president of The David Suzuki Foundation, Vancouver, British Columbia, Canada.
Iona V. Campagnola - Broadcaster, former federal cabinet minister and past president of the Liberal party, Courtenay, British Columbia, Canada.
Johnny Esaw - Vice-president, Broadcast Services, of the Edelman Houston Group, Toronto, Ontario, Canada.
Barbara Coultish - Founder & president of Barbara Coultish Talent and Model Management, Victoria, B.C., Canada.
John Baglow, M.A., Ph.D. - Writer, Trade Unionist, Ottawa, Canada.
Rita Mae Brown - Author, Afton, Virginia, U.S.A.

John Crispo, Ph.D. - Professor of Political Economy, Faculty of Management, University of Toronto, Ontario, Canada

Michael Walker - Economist, journalist, broadcaster, consultant, university lecturer and public speaker. Executive Director of The Fraser Institute, Vancouver, B.C., Canada.

Gerald Greenwald - Chairman/CEO of United Airlines, Chicago, Illinois, U.S.A.

Norman Rebin - Entrepreneur, corporate trainer/consultant, Altona, Ontario, Canada.

Lance J. Strauss - President of Lance J. Strauss Enterprises, Inc. Carmel, California, U.S.A.

Lawrence Iwasaki - Award-winning hairdresser, Proprietor of Maison Lawrence Hair Salon, Burnaby, B.C., Canada.

William E. Simon - Former Secretary of the Treasury (USA), Morristown, New Jersey, U.S.A.

Yassemi Mehranguiz - Painter, Tehran, Iran.

Jorge Salazar-Carrillo - Economist, director of the Department of Economics, Florida International University, U.S.A.

Ed McMahon - Broadcaster, television personality and president of Ed McMahon Productions, California, U.S.A.

Denton A. Cooley, M.D. - Surgeon-in-chief, Texas Heart Institute, Houston, Texas, U.S.A.

Pierre Diouf - Senegalese ambassador to Canada, Ottawa, Canada.

Sir Richard Branson, entrepreneur; Chairman, Virgin Group, UK.
- Branson Takes Risks
- Be a lover of knowledge
- Be prepared to walk away
- Start small

Karel Husa - Conductor, Ithaca, New York, U.S.A.

Barry Morris Goldwater - Former senator, Republican candidate for President of the United States of America, 1964.

Eleanor J. Smith - Chancellor of University of Wisconsin - Parkside, U.S.A.

The Honourable Jean Charest, C.P. - Member of Parliament for Sherbrooke, Quebec; 29th Premier of Quebec Province, Canada.

Dr. Norman E. Borlaug - Nobel prize winner, Distinguished professor of International Agriculture, Texas A & M University, College Station, Texas, U.S.A.

Carol Columbus-Green - Women's control garment designer, former fashion model, president of Laracris Inc., Chicago, Illinois, U.S.A.

Dr. Nalin J. Unakar - Professor of Biological Sciences, Oakland University, Rochester, Michigan, U.S.A.

Gladys Styles Johnston, chancellor of University of Nebraska at Kearney, U.S.A.

Sir Georg Solti, music director laureate, Chicago Symphony Orchestra, Chicago, Illinois, U.S.A.

Constance Tomkinson (Lady Weeks) - Author, Chichester, West Sussex, England.

Dr. C.K Chou - Former Director of City of Hope National Medical Center, Duarte, California, U.S.A.

CHAPTER THIRTEEN 177
LEAVING YOUR FOOTPRINTS ON THE SANDS OF TIME
Selfish or Selfless? - An easy way to unload your stress - Beyond the fancy car - Your legacy - The world awaits your contribution

Bibliography 180

Index 182

Resources 187

1

SELF-EXAMINATION
An Essential First Step

The unexamined life is not worth living. - Plato / Socrates

Take an honest look at yourself. It's likely that if you had achieved all your goals, you wouldn't be reading this book. But you need to congratulate yourself because you've taken the first essential step to moving on and improving your present condition.

Self-examination is necessary. You need to ask yourself some hard questions if you really care about turning the stuff of your dreams into reality. Maybe right now you feel trapped in some dead-end job and your dream has always been to be an actor. Or you may be gainfully employed — in a job you hate! Or maybe you are working so hard that there's no time for you to enjoy yourself. In a nutshell, your present circumstance is not synonymous with happiness. In other words, you don't yet consider yourself the success that you desire to be.

What's Your Blueprint For Success?

Some people feel quite sure that if they make a lot of money they will be happy or that if they achieve their dreams, happiness will automatically follow. This book does not purport to hold the secret to your happiness. What it will do is give you a blueprint that can help you to achieve your goals -- to fulfill your dreams.

Why do you think you are not yet the person you would like to be? So many things conspire to hold you back from achieving your goals. Some of these obstacles may be your own fears, lack of persistence or drive, lack of self-discipline or self-esteem, lack of education, hazy and undefined goals, lack of proper role models, lack of commitment, unwillingness to sacrifice, or lack of talent in a particular field. This book focuses on how you can turn these obstacles and others around to create success and mastery in your life.

The motto of the Boy Scouts is "Be Prepared." A simple maxim and very true. You have to be prepared to make changes in your life if this book is going to be of any benefit to you. And that's where most people fail. When they look at where they are in the present to where they may want to be in five or ten years, there seems to be such a big gulf that they just can't bring themselves to make the kinds of changes necessary to reach their desired goals.

Time Is Your Ally

Think about this: if you're overweight, for instance, what would you say about a new diet plan advertising that it can make you lose twenty pounds in five minutes? Impossible? Or for a student, how about a revolutionary new method of learning that can help you earn a Ph.D. only hours after graduating from high school? Ridiculous, isn't it?

The fact is that the one thing you have on your side — that everyone has in equal amounts -- is time. Even though technology may not be advanced enough to help you lose weight in minutes or to acquire a university degree within hours, if you apply yourself steadily to the task, in time, you will achieve your goal. Time is your ally. Quite simply, if you know how to use your time wisely, there is no reason you can't achieve in due course any goal you set for yourself.

The so-called secret of success is really no secret at all. Simply put, it boils down to the following three statements:
- a) Know what you want and set your goal
- b) Find a method to achieve that goal
- c) Persist in working your plan until you achieve your goal

You've probably heard words to the folllowing effect:
> Little drops of water
> make a mighty ocean
> Little grains of sand
> make a mighty desert

This means that if you plan to achieve something and you begin putting in effort now towards reaching that goal, as long as you pursue that goal zealously, one day you are bound to meet with success. It applies whether you want to pursue a law degree or feel the sands of Timbuktu beneath your feet. Although time is always on your side, it does keep marching on, so the sooner you begin working towards your goals and the more consistently you do so, the better for you.

Prepare for Greatness puts the onus of your success on you, the reader. No one is responsible for your success but you. If you've been counting on someone to rescue you and carry you off on a magic carpet to the land of success, think again.

Medical doctors spend many years in preparation for their career, learning the skills they need to be the healers of society, and they are generally respected for their learning and expertise. Would you rather take your fibrillating heart to someone who woke up one morning and declared himself a doctor without the benefit of any training? Of course not. Although the successful medical doctor has reason to feel satisfied with his abilities, this is not to say that medical doctors must all be happy people. Let's not confuse the achievement of one's goals with happiness. In the United States, for example, medicine has one of the highest suicide and divorce rates of any profession. Happiness, remember, lies within.

Some of the happiest people you would ever meet may be living somewhere in simple huts with just a patch of land on which to grow their crops. Yet, they may know the joy of living and may be much happier than a movie star doing three-martini lunches in Hollywood. Still, the sweet scent of success summons us.

Success has been appropriately defined as the progressive realization of worthy goals. If you are not sure about what you want in life, you should be thinking seriously about setting pen to paper to clarify your goals. People spend days planning a trip to ensure that it's a success, or they put in a lot of hours planning a family picnic. When it comes to mapping out a plan for life's journey, however, the same people are willing to leave it to the uncertainties of circumstance and chance. What prevents people from writing down their goals? Is it laziness or perhaps an inability to see any correlation between crystallizing goals on paper and their eventual realization? If you don't have your goals written down, consider carefully the reasons why you have not done so. Is it a fear of not being able to live up to your aspirations? Or is it that you are among the majority of people who are not sure what they actually want out of life?

Does The Pursuit Of Happiness Pay?

What does make people happy? What makes you happy? Mihaly Csikszentmihalhyi, Ph.D., of the University of Chicago published a book in 1990 after twenty-five years of asking: What makes people happy? Csikszentmihalyi interviewed hundreds of people all over the world including chess masters, business executives, athletes, artists, writers, janitors, and asked them all to recall what gave them their happiest moments. What do you think was the winning response? Exquisitely prepared food? Sex, booze and rock and roll? None of those. The answer most people gave was simple: Work.

Csikszentmihalyi writes in his book, *Flow: The Psychology of Optimal Experience:*

> *The best moments usually occur when a person's body or mind is stretched to its limit in a voluntary effort to accomplish something difficult or worthwhile. Such experiences are not necessarily pleasant at the time. The swimmer's muscles might have ached during his most memorable race, his lungs might have felt like exploding, and he might have been dizzy with fatigue — yet these could have been the best moments of his life.*

Csikszentmihalyi describes this phenomenon as "flow," a state characterized by total absorption in work, and pride in achievement. In this state, people exceed their own best efforts in quality and quantity of work.

Have you discovered what inspires you to maximize your efforts?

Clarify Your Dreams

What is the goal that most inspires you? What would you most like to be doing with your life? What are your dreams? If you aren't sure, then it's about time you clarified that for yourself. You can't achieve your goal if you don't yet know what it is.

Success coach Anthony Robbins phrases the question this way: "What would you do with your life if you were sure that there was no way you could fail in pursuing that goal?" Would you be a pilot, lawyer, professional speaker, university professor, world traveller, entrepreneur, actor, writer, scientist, an inventor, astronaut, painter, concert pianist, talk show host, journalist, linguist, clown, cook, or an engineer? Think about it.

Write Down Your Goals And Follow Through

Now whatever it is that you aspire to do with your entire life, or any portion of it, you had better get it down on paper and set your mind to it so strongly that you cannot help but begin working towards its achievement. Understand that you are going to have to clear some obstacles that separate you from your goal.

Impediments to success may come in any number of forms. Do you lack the funds you need to start a business of your own or to go back to school? Others have acquired education in spite of this or have found legitimate ways to acquire the funds they need to make their dreams a reality. It can be done. You can do it too. Fear of failure may be preventing you from taking the kinds of calculated risks you need to break away from your current cycle. If that's the problem, be assured that you can conquer your fears and empower yourself for personal accomplishment. Others have done so.

Is your major weakness a lack of persistence? Imagine running in a ten-kilometer race. At the starting gun, you take the immediate lead. Everyone else is way behind you. In record-setting time, you've already covered nine kilometers. The crowd is cheering. The photographers are snapping away. You are about to get your fifteen minutes of fame. Nine kilometres. You are running faster and faster. Ten metres to the finish line, you stop abruptly — and lie down. The crowd is shouting at you: "Finish off, finish off, finish off." You can't be persuaded. Only you know how tired you feel. You can't risk it anymore. You need your rest. Five minutes later, the other runners pass you by and go through the finish line. If you had persisted a little longer, you would have won the race. So many people abandon their dreams when just a little more persistence may have meant the difference between failure and success, when just a bit more persistence may have converted potential into achievement. Make persistence your personal friend and follow through with your dreams.

Know Thy Talent

Another obstacle that may stand between you and your dreams is that you are not taking full advantage of your skills. How so?

Do you know what your gifts are? Have you thought about what your talents are? Learning and mastery are mostly functions of time. Some people learn extremely fast and we call them gifted or talented. For instance, a child prodigy may learn to play Tchaikovsky's *Nutcracker* after hearing it for a short time. Another child with an interest in music may learn the rudiments of music as a child, take more music lessons in high school, go on further to the Juilliard School of Music and graduate as a concert pianist who then plays the *Nutcracker* flawlessly at the age of 32. Yet another person may have a slight interest in music, enjoy good music on occasion, but never have the inkling to try his hand at any instrument. Instead, he goes to work as a painter and earns a good living. After a lifetime of enjoying some of the greatest musical performances of the classical masters, he begins to take lessons. Slowly, painfully, he learns piece after piece until on his eightieth birthday, he plays a passable rendition of *The Nutcracker*. All three persons at some point in their lives were able to play Tchaikovsky, but each had a different learning curve. Think about how much more difficult it would have been for player number three to have decided to make his living as a concert pianist.

People have different talents and it is wise to determine what yours are and how to cultivate them. It might have taken Michelangelo a whole lifetime to be able to run as fast as Jesse Owens! Similarly, Jesse Owens might have needed a whole lifetime to be the best poor imitation of Michelangelo. This is simply a function of individual talents. While attitude is important, the obstacle to your success may be that you are not giving enough attention to your aptitudes. Know where your talents lie and develop yourself in these areas.

According to Dr. Ben Carson, author of *Think Big*, "People who fail in life are people who find lots of excuses. It's never too late for a person to recognize that they have potential in themselves."

Recognizing that you have potential is only one part. Converting this potential into real achievement is where the next great challenge lies.

Be A Master Of Your Dreams

Most major achievements begin as only a dream in someone's mind, but it is also possible to dream forever without ever seeing anything come to fruition. You need to understand that you have to work to make your dreams a reality. Successful people, and those who aspire to success, can't afford to reside too long in dreamland. They are driven to succeed and cultivate the discipline necessary to make things happen. The step beyond thought is ACTION.

Say To Yourself, "I Can And I Will"

You must believe in yourself. If you are full of doubts about your own potential, it's unlikely that you'll develop the resilience necessary to succeed in the game of life. If you have to go around asking everybody else whether they think you can be an inventor, a writer, a doctor, or a lawyer, then you're shortchanging yourself. You do not have a strong enough sense of yourself and your capabilities. The sooner you work to change this, the better off you'll be.

Who Needs An Education?

Since there are many successful people who have never had the benefit of a college education, it's easy to dismiss education as a necessary component for success. The truth is that people learn in different ways. The high school dropout who happens to run the best restaurant in your city may have learned more about restaurant management and cooking from his own direct experience than you'll ever learn in a lifetime within the confines of a college or university.

American broadcaster Larry King is fond of saying, "I've never been to college" yet do you know how voraciously he read as a child and how much he reads and analyzes his own work to this day? He is a lifelong learner. Seminars, trade journals, reading books in your field of interest, and actually learning by doing — these are just some of the ways people learn. Give serious thought to developing the mental apparatus that God has seen fit to give you. Use your mind to help you progress.

The mind is a powerful instrument. Make it a point to dream often but as Kipling implies in his poem *If*, don't make dreams your master. Don't let the dreaming be an end in itself. Be a dreamer and a doer. Use your powers of visualization as mental preparation for transforming your visions into reality. If you want to be a great public speaker, dream about it. See yourself giving the best public speeches of your life, complete with gestures and vocal variety. Accept applause gracefully; acknowledge the standing ovation. See yourself performing your best from beginning to end. Visualization is a practical exercise and a prelude to great accomplishments. Just make sure that following the vision, there comes ACTION.

Imitate The Best — Emulate The Great

Think of examples of people whom you admire who excel at what they do, people you wish you resembled, if not in flesh, at least in personality or achievement. You may even want to surpass your role model, but first it helps to know of people whose examples inspire you to do your best. Abraham Lincoln has been the role model for many a man and woman who aspires to a leadership role. Or think of business leaders such as Lee Iacocca of Chrysler fame and Akio Morita, co-founder of Sony. No matter what your aspiration, there must be someone in the field who comes close to embodying the model of achievement you strive to emulate. Imitate the best, emulate the great, and you will go far. You may even surpass your own best ideal of yourself.

Learn The Magic Of Commitment

To succeed at anything you have to make a commitment to it. You can't forever be the dabbler and hope to rise magically to the top. What do you want to be? What do you want to do? Once you've made the decision, understand that to achieve your goal you must be totally committed. If you want to know the meaning of commitment, think of a person like Nelson Mandela who, after spending twenty-seven years in a South African jail remained unbroken in spirit and lived to become President of the country.

Be Willing To
Pay The Price Of Success

But are you willing to pay the price? When you set your eyes on that beautiful dress, new car or whatever catches your fancy in a shop, you don't go to the manager and ask whether you can have it for free, do you? The shopkeeper expects you to pay for it. You pay the price. Similarly, for whatever you set your heart upon, you must understand that you are going to have to make sacrifices. If you're a scientist, time that you could spend laughing and talking with friends may have to be sacrificed for long grueling hours in the laboratory. If you're a writer, time that could be spent working on your tan on the beach may have to be spent reading or writing. Time that you could otherwise spend engaged in frivolous activities may have to be accounted for wisely, if you want to achieve your dream.

> **If I had eight hours
> to chop down a tree
> I'd spend six sharpening my axe.**
> - Abraham Lincoln

THE PREPARATION GAME

List **three** goals you most want to achieve in your life. Go easy on yourself. A few things at a time. Know the value of contentment as you go from one goal to the next. Devise a plan for achieving each goal. Example: I would like to visit the Great Wall of China in August of next year. To make this possible I'd have to raise $2000 by the beginning of that month and be able to take three weeks away from work.

1._____

_____

_____

2._____

_____

_____

3._____

_____

_____

Example of plan to achieve goal: In order for me to raise the $2000 needed for my China trip I am going to find an additional ten hours of work per week for four months. Also I'll inform my employer next week about my plans and keep reminding her at regular intervals so that I can take three weeks off without inconveniencing my employer or myself (I don't particularly want to be fired).

* Here is my plan for achieving goal #1:
_____
_____
_____
_____

* Here is my plan for achieving goal #2:
_____
_____
_____
_____

* Here is my plan for achieving goal #3:
_____
_____
_____
_____

Note below what keeps you from achieving your goals. Knowing what may be standing in the way of your success is an essential step to turning things around. Put pen to paper right now. The first three items on the list below may be used to trigger your memory, although they may not apply to your particular case. Challenge yourself with this exercise.

1. Fear of failure

2. Lack of confidence

3. Lack of knowledge/insufficient education

4._____

5._____

6._____

7._____

8._____

9._____

10._____

Congratulations on completing this important step. Now remember that time is your ally. You won't be able to overcome all your anxieties and fears with the snap of a finger, but whip them you will.

PERSONAL PLEDGE

* I understand that time is not about to stand still for me, so the sooner I begin working to achieve my goals the better. I have no time to waste.

* I commit myself to doing all the exercises in this book and following through on the plans to achieve my goals.

* I further understand that preparation is paramount to my success. I will find out how best to prepare myself to achieve my goals.

POINTS TO PONDER

* Will the achievement of the goals listed above make me a happier person?

* Do I truly want to commit myself to fulfilling these dreams?

* Will the pursuit of these goals bring out the best in me?

* What would I do with my life if my success were guaranteed?

Signature:_____

Date:_____

> **I know of no more encouraging fact than the unquestionable ability of man to elevate his life by a conscious endeavor.**
> - Henry David Thoreau, American writer

SUCCESS TIPS:
RICHARD McCORMICK, CEO, U.S. West Inc., Englewood, Colorado, U.S.A.

My success has been a combination of education, experience, hard work, being in the right place at the right time, having the right mentors and just plain good luck.

The one thing that I always stress, though, is being prepared to take advantage of opportunities.

Early in my career, I was given an assignment to prepare and present to several top company officials. The subject was a rather mundane engineering issue, something that really didn't interest me much. Even so, I worked my tail off preparing and practicing for that briefing.

Only later did I find out that the briefing was really a test -- being given to several others who had been assigned the same task. The others evidently hadn't taken it seriously and their presentations showed it. Mine was judged the best. I was told later that my career got a jump-start that day. I've always remembered the lesson I learned: Be prepared -- do your best no matter how unimportant the task may seem. You never know who'll be watching.

Success to me also means meeting the demands of my job, while insisting on a fairly normal family life!

> **To fear is one thing.**
> **To let fear grab you by the tail**
> **and swing you around is another.**
>
> - Katherine Paterson, *Jacob Have I Loved* (1980)

2

CONFRONT YOUR FEARS

**Courage is the first of human qualities
because it is the quality
that guarantees all others.**
- Sir Winston Churchill

When you allow your fears to lead the way, you permit success to flee in haste.
In William Shakespeare's *Julius Caesar* Mark Antony intones,

> Cowards die many times before their death
> The valiant never taste of death but once

Many have 'died' at the thought of going back to school to upgrade their skills after several years of raising a family. We've all 'died' at the thought of actually following through with our dreams: To travel around the world, learn to fly a plane, learn to dance the tango, learn to confront the computer, build a home of our own, or learn to speak in public.

If you've experienced pangs of distress at the thought of breaking out of your current mold into a new and uncharted area, be assured that you are in good company. Many people share these fears.

Prepare To Conquer Fear

You may be saying to yourself, "I am a slow learner" or "I am too nervous to be any good at public speaking." Forget it. You can prepare yourself to improve your performance dramatically — in whatever you want to do. Garner the courage, plunge in, and soon you'll have a record of success behind you upon which to build even more successes.

Banish Your Fear Of Failure; Clear The Way For Success

Fear of failure is perhaps the most insidious of all the fears that prevent people from trying. If we can confront and banish the fear within ourselves, it will become easier to face and conquer external obstacles. According to an African proverb: "If you can conquer the enemy within, the enemy outside can do you no harm." The thought of being rejected after a job interview can be paralyzing to a job seeker. The thought of not being chosen for a part in a play may strike fear into the heart of a budding young star. The very thought of making a fool of oneself at the lectern means that many people will never experience the thrill of communicating their ideas to an audience. Likewise, fear of success may be just as insidious. Fear of success may sabotage your own attempts to succeed. If you constantly think that you will not be able to handle the responsibilities that come with being successful, with every step you take forward you inadvertently take a few steps back. Not surprisingly, if you let your fears overwhelm you, you won't arrive at the place where deep down in your heart you want to go.

Pursue Excellence, Not Perfection

If you don't give yourself permission to fail, you may never have the pleasure of seeing one of your ideas come to fruition. You are only human. Don't expect perfection. If the Wright brothers had waited to make the perfect airplane before presenting their invention to the world, they would have had a long wait. You should always do the best work you are capable of, while remembering that there is a point at which you should have the courage to let go. Don't let the notion of perfectionism hold your talents hostage. You can always go on to develop and refine your project after you have subjected it to initial public scrutiny. And some of the ideas you end up using to improve your work may even come from others and not from yourself.

Let Courage Rule

Take courage and action and once your project is in progress, simply ensure that you do things the best way you know how. Of course, it doesn't hurt to do as much ground work as possible before you plunge into an activity.

You need courage to dispel the fears that bedevil and prevent you from trying. Fear is an unpleasant emotion caused by your own expectation or awareness of danger ahead. The only way you can conquer this fear is by exercising tenacity. This book is not about taking foolish risks. The message is that your dreams are attainable; however, beyond this awareness, you must devise a way of reaching your goals.

It takes courage to achieve anything in this world, even many of the things that seem to be a part of the natural cycle of life. It takes courage to commit yourself to another person in marriage, to bring children into this world and raise them to adulthood, to start your own business, or to pound the pavement looking for a job. It takes fortitude to be your own person, to be true to yourself, and to introduce new ideas into a system where people are comfortable with their own views and interpretations of truth.

It certainly took courage for Galileo to hold to the Copernican theory that the sun is the center of our solar system at a time when it was uniformly believed that Earth was the center of the universe. It took courage for Thomas Edison, once labeled an educational misfit, to develop his inventive genius, eventually patenting a record 1,093 inventions. It took courage for Mahatma Gandhi to spearhead the challenge to British rule in India and to impress his idea of nonviolence upon a historical epoch. These three people were not angels with superhuman strength or willpower, but rather they were just as human as you are. They were subject to the same fears that may now be holding you back, but they never allowed their fears to paralyze them into inaction. Remember: when you allow your fears to lead the way, you permit success to flee in haste!

Unlike Edison, it may not be your calling to advance the cause of modern technology, but no matter what your goals are, you'll profit from the spirit of Edison and others like him. Unlike Gandhi, it may not fall upon you to challenge an empire as great as the British in its former glory, but you may need to challenge yourself. Abandon the self-limiting habits you've cultivated over the years and strike out with a new sense of the possible.

How often we make a New Year's resolution and fail to follow through! Make every day the beginning of a new year and resolve now to do the things you've always wanted. If you do this, you won't be saying in the future: "I wish I had learned to read Greek;" "I wish I had learned to scuba dive;" "I wish I had started my own business;" "I wish I had travelled to see the magic and majesty of the Fijian islands."

Meet Sandra Kurtzig - MANMAN'S Girl

Sandra Kurtzig, founder of ASK Computer Systems, could have chosen to analyze her possibilities to the point of paralysis when she began to consider taking the entrepreneurial route.

In her book, *CEO: Building a $400 Million Company From The Ground Up*, Kurtzig asserts:

> ...you can succeed...if you believe in yourself, if you're optimistic and enthusiastic, persistent and curious, use common sense, work hard, and ask for what you want. Add humor to the equation - to deal with challenges and disappointments, to keep from taking yourself too seriously, and sometimes to mask your more serious intention - and you can't miss.

Does Kurtzig sound like an intrepid Silicon Valley whiz-kid magically catapulted to success? Well, let's go back to 1971 when Kurtzig was a working wife with plans of starting a family. Admittedly, by age 20, Kurtzig held a Master's degree in aeronautical and astronautical engineering, but she was employed as a salesperson for GE Computer Timesharing Service which sold time on a computer mainframe to companies such as those that needed to do complex financial analyses.

On one of her sales calls, Kurtzig met Larry Whitaker, a budding entrepreneur, who with a partner had just started Halcyon Communications. Whitaker wasn't in the market for prepackaged software such as Kurtzig was marketing for GE Computer

Timesharing Service. He wanted a program that was designed to his own specifications, a custom program, that is. Whitaker challenged Kurtzig to undertake the writing of the software herself. He went so far as to suggest that she quit her GE job and join the growing ranks of free-wheeling entrepreneurs.

Kurtzig considered the situation carefully and with the $2000 she had earned from successfully writing Whitaker's program, she launched herself as a contract programmer.

Kurtzig eventually created MANMAN, a manufacturing management program that for a long while was de rigueur for manufacturing companies both in the U.S. and abroad. The MANMAN program became the cornerstone of the multimillion dollar success story, ASK Computer Systems.

It was with courage that Kurtzig built what eventually became a $400 million dollar company in a field once dominated by males. Here is some more advice from Kurtzig to budding entrepreneurs:

> *My first advice to the aspiring entrepreneur is to think about what you like to do - a hobby, for example, that you can turn into a business - since whatever business you do go into, you'll have to love it to give it the time, dedication, and nurturing it will demand. Also don't go into business with the idea of getting rich quick. Keep in mind that the reason that instant success stories make headlines is precisely because they are so rare. More than likely, your success will be some time in coming....My final piece of advice...as an entrepreneur, you have to be ready to fail as much as you are eager to succeed. And you have to learn and grow from that failure. My story, and the story of so many others like me, is one of resurrecting successes out of failures, rather than a continuous stream of big wins. But if you meet setbacks and disappointments and challenges and confront them with the same excitement and passion that you bring to your original ideas, you can transcend them to enjoy the fruits of your labors. That's been my experience, and I sincerely believe it can be yours.*

Take Action Now!

The time for you to begin putting your plans into effect is now. To achieve your goals and enjoy the feeling of greatness that often accompanies a job well done, you need to start somewhere. The time to start is not some other day — it is now. If you don't have the courage to write down your goals now, might it also pose a problem for you to overcome the more daunting challenges that separate you from your major goals in life? Take note that every little effort you put toward your goal brings you closer to the finale.

Find The Powerful Antidote To Fear

The only antidote to fear is confrontation with all the courage you can muster. If you fear the dark, confront it — soon and often — and in time you may even fall in love with the silent music of the dark. If you have a fear of flying, accept the fact that you can conquer this fear and fly. Franklin D. Roosevelt, in his first inaugural address of 1933, said that "the only thing we have to fear is fear itself." How true. Don't nurture your fears but rather actively seek ways to overcome them. It takes courage to begin an endeavor and to continue to grow in the face of all the obstacles that will inevitably confront you as you go along.

Nothing gives you as much courage to confront a challenge as does proper preparation. You have a job interview? Don't dress up for success and then go mentally unprepared. Have a practice session with a friend. Let your friend ask you some of the questions you are likely to encounter at the interview and actually craft your answers to impress upon your potential employer your ability to handle the responsibilities of the job. Preparation is a complete experience; look at all the components of your goal and prepare yourself appropriately for each part. Confront your fears with preparation -- and transcend them.

Public speaking is a terrifying experience for many people, yet for a public speaking situation nothing equips you so well as preparation. This is not hard to figure out. Without adequate preparation, it's not too surprising if you fail to impress your audience. The only good thing that can come out of such failure is that you'll understand the wisdom of preparation for the next time.

When preparing for a speech, don't be half-hearted about it. If you want spontaneity in your speech, plan for it. Prepared spontaneity sounds like a contradiction in terms, but many of the best communicators and performers do just that. When was the last time you watched a good movie? A lot of effort and preparation goes into bringing a script to screen. A lot of time is spent on rehearsals. Even so, sometimes, more than a dozen takes are made to capture the scene to fit the director's vision. And yet, the performances are not any less enjoyable because they've been well rehearsed. In fact, you might be inclined to ask for your money back at the box office if the actors in a movie appeared not to have done their homework well. Be prepared. To professional performers, preparation is indispensable; they sometimes go to extraordinary lengths to ensure their readiness for a performance. Why not learn from the professionals? Your life is no less important.

Take A Cue From Howard Thurston, Showman Extraordinaire

Howard Thurston, born in Columbus, Ohio, on July 20, 1869, is said to have led the greatest magic show in history. Thurston had the courage to go for his dreams while admitting that there were many magicians who knew more about magic than he. Two secrets of his success were reported by Dale Carnegie in his book *Five Minute Biographies*: firstly, Thurston "had the ability to put his personality across the footlights. He was a master showman, he knew human nature and he said this quality was just as important for a magician as a knowledge of magic." No gesture, intonation, or lifting of an eyebrow was a matter of accident. Secondly, "he loved his audience and they could tell. Before the curtain went up, he stood in the wings saying: 'I love my audience. I love to entertain them. I've got a grand job. I'm so happy! I'm so happy!'"

Howard found something that he loved to do and threw himself into it, not thinking about the money he could make, but the service he could render to his audience. The audience must have kept coming back not only because of his skill but also the sense that here was someone who truly loved to make them happy.

TIPS FOR BOOSTING COURAGE

* Confront your fears. Take action, and soon enough you will have a record of success behind you to bolster your spirits when doubts assail you.

* Failure is just a part of the learning process. If you think about it carefully, you'll realize that even in fields in which you excel you may have had a setback or two at some point. Don't be paralyzed by the fear of failure.

* Good preparation will help cast away your fears.

* If you wait until everything in your life is perfect before taking action toward attaining your goals, you may have a long wait. Begin now!

* Strive to do your best. Leave perfection to the Creator. Pursue excellence.

* It takes courage to be involved in life. What do Galileo Galilei, Mahatma Gandhi, and Thomas Edison have in common? They had the courage of their convictions and acted on their beliefs. If they had not been determined, their names would not be known to us today.

* The only effective cure for fear is meeting it head-on with all the courage you can muster.

> **You must do
> the thing
> you think
> you cannot do.**
>
> - Eleanor Roosevelt

EXERCISE FOR BOOSTING COURAGE

List three of your fears.

1._____

2._____

3._____

For each fear above, write down how you're going to prepare yourself to confront it. For example: "To overcome my fear of public speaking, I will enroll in a communications course at my local community college."

1._____

2._____

3._____

Say "I Will" To Your Dreams

Have you resolved to reach for your goals? Have you summoned the courage to say, "I will" to your dreams? You must break out of your comfort zone and reach out for the "new worlds" that lie beyond your immediate reach. Once you are on the road toward achieving your goals, be careful not to sabotage yourself by losing sight of your dream. Don't buckle under the pressure of hardships; instead, endure and you will master your troubles. In the words of English poet John Milton, 'have the courage never to submit or yield' to defeat.

> **Opportunity does not come to those who wait.
> It is captured by those who attack.**
> - General Douglas MacArthur

3

MAKE PERSISTENCE YOUR FRIEND

> Nothing in the world
> can take the place of persistence.
> Talent will not;
> nothing is more common
> than unsuccessful men with talent.
> Genius will not;
> unrewarded genius is almost a proverb.
> Education will not;
> the world is full of educated derelicts.
> Persistence and determination alone
> are omnipotent.
> — Calvin Coolidge

How many times did you have to take your driver's test before you obtained your license? If you had failed five times, would you have given yourself another chance? You would not have given up, accepting grimly that you were just not cut out to drive a car. No, even after many failures, you'd continue learning and taking the test until you passed, right?

Tony Robbins asks a question that perfectly illustrates the meaning of persistence: How often do you allow a baby to attempt walking before you give up on it and say that perhaps it wasn't meant to walk? Absurd? Exactly.

How many times would you have to take an examination for professional certification before you gave up, thinking you were not meant to succeed in that field? It is not uncommon for some lawyers to pass the bar exam after more than one try. In fact, while it is ideal to pass on the first try, it is no news that some top legal eagles passed after the second or even third try. It takes persistence to keep studying for an exam as grueling as the bar exam. The following story of Maxcy Filer, attorney-at-law, is a perfect illustration of the results of persistence.

Maxcy Filer, Attorney-at-law
Learns A Lesson From Persistence

When Maxcy Filer first took the California bar exam, he was 36 and freshly out of law school. Although he failed on the first try, he did not give up on his dream to become a lawyer. He tried again — and failed. Since the California Bar can be taken twice a year at six-month intervals, Filer figured that sooner or later he would pass. Well, he tried again for the third time -- and failed. Not to worry, he tried a fourth time. No luck!

Mr. Filer, born in Marianna, Arkansas, had worked as a dental technician before moving to California in 1952. Once in California, Filer took an interest in the civil rights movement that was just beginning to grow. He wanted to make a difference, but he realized that in his new life as a milkplant loader and parking lot attendant, he was limited in how much he could contribute. Law school beckoned and so at the age of 32, Filer enrolled in the now-defunct Van Norman Law School in Los Angeles. Following his graduation, Filer did clerkships for the Compton and Los Angeles city attorneys, researching and writing briefs. Every six months following, he tried the California bar exam. And each time, he failed. Filer, however, continued studying for the exams. Eventually Filer had failed the California bar exam so often that whenever the envelope arrived from the examining body, he postponed opening it for as long as possible. Then one day, after failing 47 times, he actually passed -- twenty-four years after he had first taken the California bar exam. He says, "I never once thought seriously about giving up — I absolutely knew that sooner or later I would pass that exam." And he did. By that time two of his sons, Kelvin and Anthony, had finished law school and passed the bar exam, Kelvin on his first attempt. Filer became an attorney and a partner in a law firm run by his son Kelvin.

Filer's example illustrates that if you want something badly enough, and you persist long enough, there's no reason why success should not eventually greet you for your efforts.

Never Give Up

Maxcy Filer kept his goal perpetually in view and so should you. Giving up is too easy. Winston Churchill is of course the great statesman who, after a lifetime of service to his native Britain, is assessed in the *New Encyclopaedia Britannica* thus:

> *In any age and time a man of Churchill's force and talents would have left his mark on events and society. A gifted journalist, a biographer and historian of classic proportions, an amateur painter of talent, an orator of rare power, a soldier of courage and distinction, Churchill by any standards, was a man of rare versatility. But it was as a public figure that he excelled. His experience of office was second only to Gladstone's, and his gifts as a parliamentarian hardly less, but it was as a wartime leader that he left his indelible imprint on the history of Britain and on the world. In this capacity, at the peak of his powers, he united in a harmonious whole his liberal convictions about social reform, his deep conservative devotion to the legacy of his nation's history, his unshakable resistance to tyranny from the right or from the left, and his capacity to look beyond Britain to the larger Atlantic community and the ultimate unity of Europe. A romantic, he was also a realist, with an exceptional sensitivity to tactical considerations at the same time as he unswervingly adhered to his strategical objectives. A fervent patriot, he was also a citizen of the world. An indomitable fighter, he was a generous victor. Even in the transition from war to peace, a phase in which other leaders have often stumbled, he revealed, at an advanced age, a capacity to learn and to adjust that was in many respects superior to that of his younger colleagues.*

Does this sound like a man who knew failure? Well, Churchill was no stranger to failure. His school days were marked by a poor academic record which provided justification for his father to enroll him in the Royal Military Academy, later known as Sandhurst.

Churchill did not pass the entrance examination on the first try. He tried again and failed, managing to pass only on his third attempt. Later, after having become a popular journalist, he failed three times to be voted into Parliament. He never gave up. Not Churchill.

Great Men And Women Do Know Great Pains

Persistence doesn't merely mean sticking to your goals or persevering in the face of adversity. It is keeping supreme faith in the eventual outcome of an event. Don't be bullied into submission. Don't quit because of a failure here or there. Great men and women do know great pains.

Great men and women are those adept at hiding the years of endured pain and sorrow and disappointment behind the smiles of achievement and good fortune.

Have you asked life for what you deserve? I hope you've not given up already, because you do have to keep knocking until you get results. The results are not always spectacular, but whatever results you do get should provide you with an opportunity to learn. Ask yourself, "What can I do to get results better than what I am getting now?" Of course, you are going to encounter brickwalls, but each failure should spur you on to greater things. View your mistakes and unsuccessful attempts as steps in the learning process. Use them to propel you toward your destination.

> **DON'T QUIT**
> When things go wrong as they sometimes will;
> When the road you're trudging seems all uphill;
> When the funds are low, and the debts are high
> And you want to smile; but you have to sigh;
> When care is pressing you down a bit
> Success is failure turned inside out;
> The silver tints of the clouds of doubt;
> And you never can tell how close you are;
> It may be near when it seems afar.
> So, stick to the fight when you're hardest hit
> It's when things go wrong that you mustn't quit.
> - Anonymous

Don't Lose Sight Of Your Destination

Jawaharlal Nehru, the first prime-minister of India, once said that Mahatma Gandhi had taught him that in undertaking a journey it is important not to lose sight of one's destination. Gandhi is purported to have said: "There will be many turnings along the way. It will be easy to get lost on attractive bypaths that lead nowhere. Resist deflections."

To develop the kind of tenacity or indefatigable spirit that can help you reach your goals, it is necessary to stay focused. If your goal loses its lustre, there is no incentive to strive toward making it a reality. You lose your staying power. There are countless distractions in this world, many interesting diversions that can keep you off track if you allow yourself to be distracted. You must fight the distractions by focusing on your goal. You will have to be flexible to accommodate the unexpected twists and turns that will no doubt come into play. At the same time, if you allow these to sidetrack you, you'll not have the pleasure of beginning something worthwhile and seeing it through to completion. Any one can start a race, but it takes a lot more to keep running until the finish line. You have to exercise your power of choice and focus, and believe that despite all roadblocks you will still fulfill your dream.

Having a tenacious spirit means being fully aware that as much as you would like to see yourself achieve your goals with a minimum of hassle, the reality may be much different. At some point, you will probably have to learn to cope with rejection. You'll need stamina to survive the difficulties that accompany the pursuit of an endeavour. The strength of your belief in your dream, however, is an indicator of your ability to persist and achieve it.

Any number of excuses can stand between you and the achievement of your goals. Instead of crying that circumstances are just not right, what you should be doing is finding ways to make them right. Excuses are abundant. Poverty, often used as an excuse, can also be a great motivator. A knowledge of the mean streets of poverty can move you to reach out for more prosperous avenues of personal enrichment. Now, it is true that poverty can inhibit achievement; there are a number of very real ways in which an individual's potential can be stifled. A perpetually hungry child, a child who is unable to fill her stomach is unlikley to be the child most eager to fill her mind. People who have experienced discrimination can tell you how it breeds in them anger and cynicism. The knowledge that you can be denied access to certain opportunities because of your race, colour, creed, age, gender, or background can prevent even the most talented individual from trying. From within these "disadvantaged" situations, those who do try must have great strength and courage of conviction.

For those who may be unwitting victims of discrimination, it is important to note that in every society, there are people who cannot deny their conscience, who cannot stand to see injustice and who will go against the herd to preserve their principles. It is to people such as these that the Mahatma Gandhis and Martin Luther King Jr.'s of the world have appealed in their fight to break the shackles of racism and oppression. No matter how tough life is in your own corner of the world, if you look carefully and thoroughly and make the acquaintance of people who will judge you only by your character, the avenues to success will be more open to you.

If you feel blocked by a group of people or system, you could exercise the right to seek out better opportunities elsewhere. Or if you see an opportunity for effecting change, confront the system. There is no point in torturing yourself by remaining in a discriminatory situation; fight it and win rather than succumbing until your spirit is broken and you have no power left to continue. Knowledge and determination are your greatest weapons against discrimination. If you find that you cannot evoke the evangelizing zeal of a Martin Luther King Jr. or summon the striking and penetrating logic of a Malcolm X, don't give up — you have yet another recourse to fight discrimination. Simply be the best at what you do. Make excellence your aim and you cannot fail in the long run.

If you find that your own ignorance is holding you back, you could acquire the knowledge you need to put yourself on the road to success. Make use of libraries. Check out bookstores. If you make bookstores and libraries your haunts, you'll not remain ignorant much longer. Take advantage of used bookstores, magazines, night courses, correspondence courses, college courses, and high school upgrading courses. Even in developing countries, those who really want to learn can sometimes find the means to acquire a decent education and the knowledge they need to make positive changes in their lives.

Gather knowledge and stop using your temporary ignorance as an excuse. It is said that there are more questions than answers, but that shouldn't stop you from seeking answers to the important questions in your life. If you are persistent in your search, you'll be surprised at how many answers you'll find to guide you over the common hurdles you encounter in your quest for personal fulfillment and achievement. Firstly, you need to know how to locate information -- and your local public library can be of tremendous help to you. On second thought, if you are keeping up with technology, the information you need may be at your fingertips with the use of a smart phone or a computer.

Be in active and perpetual quest for opportunity but be sure to be prepared at all times so that when the door opens you can enter with confidence.

If you are persistent in your search, sooner or later you will find your niche somewhere.

I believe in always having goals, and always setting them high.

- Sam Walton (founder of WALMART)

LESSONS FROM PERSISTENCE

* Learn from Winston Churchill and Maxcy Filer. Both failed to reach their goals a number of times but neither ever gave up. They knew what they wanted and never lost the determination to succeed - making persistence their closest friend. Follow the examples these men have set.

* Don't let any experience of failure serve to impede your success. On the way to your goals, you will encounter many obstacles and make many mistakes. Recognize these as part of the learning process and persist in your journey.

* As Gandhi says, "There will be many turnings along the way. It will be easy to get lost on attractive bypaths that lead nowhere. Resist deflections."

* If you are a victim of discrimination, note that knowledge and determination are your greatest weapons.

* Knowledge is potent. If ignorance is part of what is preventing you from succeeding in life, make books your constant companions. Learn from everything you read and apply your newfound knowledge in productive ways.

* Pledge to be relentless in the pursuit of your ideals. Maintain the courage of your convictions and persist until your efforts meet with success.

EXERCISE - ON PERSISTENCE

For your three most important goals, how long are you willing to persist in order to achieve them? Give yourself a time-frame (days, weeks, months or a specific number of years) within which you are willing to persist in your pursuit. Take this timeframe as a guide, not a rule.

Goal #1:

Time-frame:

Goal #2:

Time-frame:

Goal #3:

Time-frame:

Read on

Our greatest weakness lies in giving up. The most certain way to succeed is to always try - just one more time.
— Thomas Edison

The Dominican University Goals Study

In 2011, psychologist Dr. Gail Matthews of Dominican University, California, conducted a study on goals that confirmed what many had suspected, that writing down one's goals and telling others about the goals increased the chances that one would achieve them.

You have made the commitment to go for the gold, for your dreams. But did you put a time-frame on the attainment of your goal?

SUCCESS TIPS:

ALEX TROTMAN, Chairman and CEO, Ford Motor Company, Dearborn, Michigan, U.S.A.

For starters, know your stuff. Study hard at your chosen profession. Master its skills. Today's working world is an intensely competitive place, and knowledge is the basic price of admission.

Think and compete globally. Markets, capital, technology, information and products increasingly ignore national borders. You need to learn about other cultures -- how they think, how they communicate, how they do business. A second language is good; a third better.

Be flexible but durable. The world is changing; don't let it change without you. The ability to learn, adapt, and absorb the inevitable failures are key to staying in the race.

Know how to lead. Leadership is more than "authority"; it's courage, vision, ethics and a grounding in reality as well. Think about leadership. Read about it. Study it in the leaders you respect. It's important.

And remember, none of this works without determination. Success is not for the ambivalent. It's for those who know what they want and go after it, no matter how difficult the path.

MADELEINE STERN, proprietor, RARE BOOKS, New York, New York, U.S.A.

The most important element in success, I believe, is having a goal in the first place. So many people these days seem to be born and continue aimless.

I was fortunate since, early on, I knew pretty much what I wanted to do and persisted in trying to do it. I am still persisting.

JACKI SORENSEN, aerobic dance company executive, choreographer; Jacki's Inc., Deland, Florida, U.S.A..

Passion and persistence are keys. If I'm passionate about something I believe that whatever it is is boundless and the "goal" is therefore always out of sight over the horizon. If you don't have a true passion for whatever it is that you are doing goals are merely like days on a calendar -- something to be checked off. You must be persistent and overcome what may seem like obstacles or roadblocks thrown up by those who don't share the vision. If you are passionate, persistence comes naturally. Eventually preparation will meet opportunity and you will be "successful."

What I consider to be the greatest achievement in my lifetime actually did involve setting a goal. However, it wasn't a goal for me; it was a target for everyone I was working with. We were raising money for the Special Olympics by holding over 100 simultaneous Danceathons all over the country on one weekend. I went on the Today Show the day before this was to happen and announced that we expected to raise over $1 million. My supporters thought I was dreaming, but in the end we raised over four million dollars in those two days!

> **Nothing great is created suddenly, any more than a bunch of grapes or a fig.**
> **If you tell me that you desire a fig,**
> **I answer you that there must be time.**
> **Let it first blossom, then bear fruit, then ripen.**
> — Epictetus

4

REDISCOVER YOUR TALENTS

If a man has a talent and cannot use it, he has failed. If he has a talent and uses only half of it, he has partly failed. If he has a talent and learns somehow to use the whole of it, he has gloriously succeeded, and won a satisfaction and a triumph few men ever know.
- Thomas Wolfe

Look around you. Take a good look at the variety inherent in nature. What would it be like if all animals were made of stone and all plants composed of silica? What if the ocean itself were rockhard and the sky a massive dome of rock hanging over our heads? Absurd?

Have you ever observed a waterfall or set your eyes upon the shimmering sands of a desert? Have you been fortunate enough to see the beauty of snow-capped mountains in their frosty array? Don't we all love the variety in nature?

What Do You Do Best?

The deserts and oceans and mountains are an infinitesimal part of the variety found in nature. Let's take it a bit further into the land of absurdity. How would you react to a neighing snake? Wouldn't you jump out of your skin to hear a cock barking and a dog crowing? Barking is what a dog does best and crowing is what a cock does best. The best efforts of a crowing dog may be a disastrous imitation of even the worst crowing cock and vice versa.

Animal sounds are an innate part of the animals. Fortunately, human talents go beyond that. Humans are more versatile and have the ability to master several different skills in different fields of endeavour. An excellent pilot may also be an award-winning writer who builds miniature doll houses as a hobby. Another may be a tough-minded trial lawyer widely acclaimed for her knowledge of indigenous art, and who also plays the trumpet acceptably well every other Saturday at her local professional club.

The question has been raging for years as to whether writers are born or made. Of course no one is born with a pen in hand, but some people have the innate ability to write better than others and to develop faster with the proper training and guidance. In any case, there is always a price to be paid in time and effort. The gifted writer may have to put in long years of work to come up with the telling phrases that certify her as an expert on words and language. The less talented writer may also eventually be able to reach that same high level of skill but will have to pay a higher price. Although the price varies, the whole world of literary expression and creativity is open to anyone who cares to work hard enough to establish a foothold.

Allow Your Talents To Lead You

With the proper attitude, it is possible to learn to do practically anything; however, there is no question that because of innate talents and varying abilities, some people master certain skills faster than others. It pays to be aware of the things at which you excel. Allow your talents to lead you.

It is good to find out what your options are, but don't force yourself to do one thing if your talents are pulling you in another direction. Parents have the most to learn from this. Forcing a child to become a medical doctor because his mother is a doctor may be counterproductive in the long run. What if he wants to be a movie director and has the talent to move in that direction? What is the point of pressuring a person to become an accountant when his natural talents lead him to a career in dance or songwriting? Fortunately, we all have a range of things we can do and excel at if we put in the proper effort and maintain faith in our own capabilities. It will profit you not to stray too far from your natural abilities.

In the book *Writing to Inspire*, Lee Roddy, of Penn Valley, California, shares an important point of view:

> *I believe that people are born with the gift to write — the desire to communicate and the ability to use words on paper to express ideas. If you have these qualities, and the willingness to put time and effort into training, you can develop your skills, because technique can be learned. It's something like a diamond in the rough. It can be polished and faceted to great beauty and price, but it must have been created a diamond in the beginning.*

Abraham Lincoln
Had A Winning Way With Words

It is said that the source of Abraham Lincoln's desire for education is something of a mystery since his parents were functionally illiterate. He had only about a year of formal education, but that did not dampen his enthusiasm for education. According to neighbors, Lincoln was the kind of person who would tramp for miles to borrow a book. Although he did not have the benefit of a large library, the few books he had access to he devoured with uncommon passion. Although he worked at many different jobs, when he realized he had a winning way with words, he chose to become a lawyer. Who is to say what course history would have taken if Abraham Lincoln had not allowed himself to be drawn to where his talents and interests lay.

Michael Jackson loved to sing and dance. He had the talent for both and continually strove to improve his own performances. Louis L'Amour was in love with the written word and expressed this love in the huge body of work he left behind in the form of Western novels. Steven Spielberg loves to direct movies and has had a very successful career in the entertainment industry.

Imagine if Abraham Lincoln had decided to be a singer and dancer. Or if Michael Jackson had decided that he would be a blacksmith in spite of his voice and talents as a dancer. What if Steven Spielberg had insisted on being a marathon runner. Would they not have shortchanged themselves? For everyone there is a pull, a magnet, and you only have to pay attention to the still, small voice in your mind to be pointed in the right direction. Follow your dream; practice, persist, and become all you can be.

In some cases, a person will appear destined for a certain career, drawn to a cause with an insistence difficult to fight. If you are such a person, that is, if your talents have that much power in defining your course in life, you are quite fortunate. Look at the different alternatives available to you and exert yourself in an area that will bring you optimum professional and personal fulfillment.

You have to be careful though, that you do not allow other people to smother your talent. Don't let others define your greatness or mediocrity. Many a promising talent has been crushed by the ridicule or disbelief of others. Don't be an unwitting victim. Have enough strength and faith in yourself to transcend the negative comments of others.

**Immerse Yourself
In The Milieu Of Your Given Talent**

Once you determine the things that pull you, allow yourself to explore them fully, to find out whether the satisfaction gained from pursuing each activity is fulfilling. Take into special account the things that give you the greatest satisfaction and sense of accomplishment. Immerse yourself in the milieu of your given talent.

You cannot wish to be a lawyer and yet forever avoid reading law books. You cannot want to be a Christian so badly when you hate to read the Bible. You cannot want to be a writer and love reading while neglecting the actual writing process. Wishing alone will not make you a lawyer, a good Christian, or a compelling writer.

If you have a talent and you want to cultivate it, you must immerse yourself totally in the milieu of your desired subject. Study the best practitioners of your craft and aim to do as well and even to surpass their efforts. Keep in mind though, that you will grind yourself to a halt if you become obsessed with comparing yourself to others. Aim to compete with yourself. Aim to exceed your own best efforts. Don't let others decide the pace at which you run your life, merely use their positive actions as an example. While a hurried pace works just fine for some people, those who do things much more slowly are not necessarily lazy or lacking drive. Different people work at different paces. You don't have to drive yourself wild to accomplish the things that are dear to your heart.

Doing the things that give you the most satisfaction may mean going against the herd. But what is the point of suffering in silence as a real estate agent when all you've ever really wanted to be is a pilot? You may be stuck in your current position because of personal financial obligations. If you look hard enough, you may be able to ease yourself out of the current burden of an unfulfilling job and find something that fits more with your interests and talents while still living up to your responsibilities. Thinking, strategizing, and taking action, can get you out of many a hopeless-looking situation.

If you make money the sole criterion for defining your interests, you may in the long run fall short of achieving your cherished dreams. Better first to concentrate on perfecting your craft. For example, if you spend all your money and time on an office to set yourself up as a singer and performer and neglect to improve your voice, you'll probably impress people with the elegance of your office, but you will not capture their attention with the beauty of your voice. In this case, the office is obviously the least necessary aspect of your trade. You must decide why you are taking your chosen course of action and what your priorities are.

Be Aware Of Your Options

It is said that you are what you eat; we could also say that you are even more what you take into your mind. If you want to do something to benefit yourself or humankind in general, there is much in the way of literature to spur you on to success. However, there is also no shortage of materials that promote negative attitudes. Beware. Study should be paramount, but be selective in what you feed your mind.

If your success negatively impinges on the health or comfort of others in any way, then you've only won yourself a Pyrrhic victory. While you may still enjoy all the perks of your "success," any victory gained at the expense of others is not true success and is no way to prepare for greatness.

Developing your talents should be most important to you. God didn't put you in this world to let your talents go to waste. Take hold of your given talent and develop it with passion.

People who are passionate about their dreams, even to the point of obsession, are those who eventually end up enjoying greatness in their fields. As billionaire Bill Gates has said, "Being maniacal about something is very helpful." The little girl who loves tearing her toys apart and tries developing some great new toys of her own may be the brilliant engineering designer of tomorrow. The child who loves writing and acting in his own plays today, if he later immerses himself in the world of theatre, may succeed in dazzling audiences on Broadway.

Educate yourself about all the options available in the areas where you feel a "calling." In the end, you have the power to choose. However, if you feel pulled toward a life of crime and high intrigue, you ought to be aware of the ramifications of choosing this as your life's vocation. It's up to you to exercise the choice you have and to seek better options. Just don't allow yourself to be hemmed in by present circumstances.

When you begin to make your first tentative moves toward your goal, people may tell you what a mistake you are making. There can be so much discouragement, especially in the fields of art and music, that it is easy for the faint of heart to give up in frustration. If you are able to survive this initial discouragement and continue pursuing your dream, you will reach your goal in due course. You will prove that you really had the talent and you'll be amazed how many people will then align themselves with you and urge you to persist in reaching out for even more formidable goals. "We knew you'd make it all along," they'd say. You'd better believe it yourself first.

MOOCs to the Rescue

One of the blessings of technology in the last few decades is the spread and reach of the Internet. The vast array of educational opportunities the Internet has spawned is fast making many common excuses for lack of achievement obsolete. Can't get out on a rainy day to go to the library? No problem. The library is right there on your desktop, laptop, tablet computer, or smart phone! Can't afford to pay thousands of dollars to learn a skill? No problem. There are thousands of free courses from highly accomplished instructors or schools that you can take for little or no money.

Amazingly, it is not just a few bogus courses that are being offered online. Top-tier universities such as Harvard, Massachusetts Institute of Technology, Stanford University, and hundreds of universities around the world are vying with one another to share information that one might have had to pay thousands of dollars for in the past -- all free of charge. Or for very little money.

Sebastian Thrun, a professor at Stanford University, played a role in what has come to be known as MOOCs -- massive open online courses. In 2011, Thrun was pleasantly surprised when he opened up a course he offered at Stanford to anyone around the world who wanted to take it -- online; 160,000 individuals from over 190 countries enrolled. Not only did Thrun realize that some of his Stanford students preferred taking the class online to coming to the classroom but also he realized that Stanford did not have a monopoly on smart students.

Thrun gave up tenure at Stanford and opened an online university called Udacity. Since then, other MOOCs have popped up, inluding edx, run by Harvard and MIT, and Coursera, open to dozens of universities and growing.

There are many other websites that would help you master mathematics, for example, for free (khanacademy.org) or master a foreign language (duolingo.com). New offerings are coming up online all the time so the least you can do is make an effort to search. Do not assume that what you desire does not exist. You will be surprised to find out that someone somewhere is thinking of you and has on some small corner of the web just what you need to turn your life around. Even raising money to start a business, with online companies like Kickstarter, mean that you may not have to visit your unfriendly banker in order to raise money to start a business.

The resource section of this book (pages 187-192) provides some links to educational and entrepreneurial resources. The search engine may be an open sesame to untold riches -- in knowledge or otherwise. Go for it. But be sure that you do not dissipate your energies by running after everything that is being offered. Be selective. Focus is key, remember?

Sit In One Chair

Some people have many dreams. They feel drawn toward many things. There is nothing wrong with this, except that it is difficult to divide your attention between so many different things and still attain an equally high mastery of all. Mastery is most often a function of time, effort and quality of training. Even if you could master several different things at once, it pays to concentrate your efforts on fewer activities. Prioritize your life. What is the most important thing you want to accomplish? What are other minor things that deserve your attention? Don't give up the other dreams; you need to organize and prioritize them such that your time is going in the right places.

Do Something Well

If Martin Luther King Jr. had concentrated his efforts on leading the civil rights movement at the same time as entertaining the desire to be the best jazz trumpeter, swimmer, race car driver, and mathematician, chances are he would have fallen into well-deserved obscurity. Certainly he wouldn't have been able to leave his mark as a civil rights activist on the collective psyche of humankind.

If Gandhi had devoted as much time to playing golf as he did to promoting the cause of Indian independence, he would never have made so great an impact.

A. Lawrence Lowell, who served as president of Harvard between 1909 and 1933, instituted a new curriculum there that emphasized both "concentration and distribution." This has been adopted by most American universities, and posits that every educated person "should know a little of everything and something well." Good advice indeed. So, even as you savor the smorgasbord of life's opportunities, know your one key area for laserlike attention and focus.

Enrico Caruso Believed In His Talent

In the early 1900's, Enrico Caruso, an Italian opera star from Naples, overcame the odds to be renowned for his magical voice. From a young age, he practiced patiently and maintained an unwavering determination based on faith in his abilities and the hope that he would eventually succeed. When he began to develop his voice, it was so whispery that one teacher explained to him "kindly" that not only could he not sing but that his voice sounded like the wind in the shutters.

In *Five Minute Biographies*, Dale Carnegie tells the amazing story of that boy, Caruso, whose peasant mother went barefoot so he could develop his musical talents. For years, Caruso's voice broke when he tried to hit the high notes and his performance as an actor was so terrible that once during a performance the audience booed and hissed him off the stage. The beginning years of Caruso's singing career were so marred by disappointment that after he became wildly successful he would often burst into tears at the thought of the humiliation and disappointment he had suffered earlier on.

Caruso's mother died when he was fifteen and he preserved the memory of her in a portrait he carried with him wherever he went. She had given birth to twenty-one children. Of these, eighteen died in infancy! This peasant woman, her life marked by sorrow and poverty, sensed that if only she could sacrifice for the sake of her son, Caruso, just maybe, their lives would take a different turn some day.

Later, with tears in his eyes, Caruso would say: "My mother went without shoes in order that I might sing." Caruso's father took the boy out of school when he was ten to work in a factory. In his extra time, Caruso studied music and persisted in his training so that by the age of twenty-one he could afford to leave the factory job and support himself solely from his singing career.

He often had to sing for his supper in the neighbourhood cafe. When finally he was given the opportunity to sing in an opera, he was so nervous that his voice broke, sending him reeling from one false note to another. At last, humiliated and exhausted by his futile efforts to recapture his voice, he burst into tears and dashed out of the theatre. Even so, Caruso persisted in singing and his occasional flashes of operatic brilliance didn't go unnoticed by local impresarios.

Another evening, as a result of sudden illness, a leading tenor failed to show up for a performance. Caruso, an understudy to the tenor, was nowhere to be seen. Messengers were sent across town to find Caruso. Finally, they located him in a wine-shop, told him the news, and requested that he follow them back to the theater to fill in for the tenor. He was panting with excitement when he arrived, but just before he walked onto the stage the world around him began to spin. Caruso performed so poorly that at the end of the performance, he was fired.

The following day, he was determined to put the heartbreak and desperation of the world behind him by committing suicide. He had only enough money to buy himself a bottle of wine. He had not eaten all day; he was drinking and thinking about his last few hours of misery on earth when suddenly the door was flung wide open and in came a messenger from the opera.

"Caruso!" he cried. "Caruso, come! The people won't listen to that other tenor. They hissed him off the stage. They're shouting for you! For you, Caruso!"

"For me?" Caruso asked. "That's silly. Why, they don't even know my name."

"Of course they don't know it," the messenger shouted, "but they want you just the same. They're shouting for 'that drunkard!'"

That was the beginning of Caruso's success as an opera singer. When he died in 1921 at the age of 48 he was mourned by many nations. For many people, one of the best voices of the time was silenced forever.

Should Caruso have given up singing in favour of factory work? Think about yourself, your talents and what you want to do with your life.

I have not ceased being fearful, but I have ceased to let fear control me. I have accepted fear as a part of life, specifically the fear of change, the fear of the unknown, and I have gone ahead despite the pounding in the heart that says: turn back, turn back, you'll die if you venture too far.
- Erica Jong
The Writer on Her Work, vol. I. (1980);
Janet Sternburg, ed.

MAKE THE MOST OF YOUR TALENTS

* What do you do best? Where do your talents lie? Don't forget that the best efforts of a crowing dog may be a disastrous imitation of even the worst crowing cock. Do you crow better than you bark? Know thyself.

* Allow your talents to lead you. It pays to be aware of the things in which you naturally excel and to cultivate them.

* Immerse yourself in the milieu of your given talent. Study should stand supreme. Once you know your talents, learn how to put them to good use.

* Once you know exactly what you want in life, write it down. By writing down your goals, you are making a commitment. You may have to challenge yourself to accomplish what may seem like an unnecessary exercise -- writing down your goals.

* Writing down your goals can be a statement of faith, a marker of hope.

    It provides for a pleasing and enriching mix in society that people have different gifts and talents. If everybody could sing as well as Whitney Houston did, where would our appreciation for the beauty of her voice be? If everyone could write as well as William Shakespeare, would we appreciate the gift of his literary genius? If everyone could handle a basketball like Magic Johnson, would we still appreciate his mastery of the sport?
    Find out what your talents are. Nurture and develop them.

5

DRIVE AND SELF-DISCIPLINE

> ...discipline is the method
> of making difficult things a habit;
> it is the way of exacting in a crisis
> the performance planned in sober calm.
> - T. Morris Longsthreth

It is all well and good to have the courage to decide that you will reach for your dreams. It is great to commit yourself to a goal and to persist. It is a fine thing to know what your talents are, but you still need self-discipline to make great things happen.

Some people love to talk about all the wonderful things they want to do, but they never get around to actually doing them. Others talk about doing certain things and exert the proper effort toward their achievement. They follow through. Drive and self-discipline can fuel the kind of effort needed to accomplish goals.

You've Got To Act To Achieve

People who are driven, know the value of fantasies and daydreams, but don't allow such dreams to stand in the way of action. Action is what makes all the difference if a goal is to be achieved.

You may have the best idea for a business since McDonald's and you can get all excited about positive cash flows, franchise opportunities and the potential to retire within five years, but if you don't initiate the appropriate chain of actions, success will remain elusive.

You need to plan. You need to find out what others have done in your field. You need to have the desire to do better than whatever has been done before. It is important to remember that if you don't take action, your project will die before its birth.

**"Whatever You Can Do
Or Dream You Can, Begin It"**
    - Goethe

Drive and self-discipline are the twin engines that will propel your idea from its beginnings to completion. A driven person will attempt to look for a way to achieve her goals despite external obstacles. A driven person will not allow himself to become a slave to the television or any other distraction that prevents him from achieving his desired goals.

>THE TELLY
>The telly tells me
>To tell you to test well
>And see if it's
>Worth it to vegetate
>Each day before it
>The harm that it does you
>The Telly

True, television can sometimes be educational, but one needs to be highly selective in choosing programs. How can a person watch five hours of television every night while complaining about the lack of time he has to educate himself? If you have five hours to spare, why don't you spend it wisely in acquiring the knowledge you need for success?

It is sad how some people go through life, an hour here...an hour there, and soon the day is over. Nothing important accomplished. They bound through life, busily jumping from one thing to another but without the urge to push themselves to accomplish the things that really matter. Make every move of yours, productive.

If You Think You Have Problems, Learn From Helen Keller

We all have problems, but Helen Keller really had problems. When you put your own problems in the proper perspective, you may find that things are not as gloomy as you thought.

Everyone has problems and there is always someone less fortunate than you. See your problems as hurdles separating you from your goals, but don't see them as insurmountable.

Helen Keller was blind and yet she read hundreds of books, more than most people with two seeing eyes can say for themselves. She wrote at least seven books of her own. Helen Keller even made a motion picture in which she played a part.

For one who also had no capacity for oral communication during most of the first nine years of her life, it is truly outstanding that Helen Keller went on to become a successful lecturer who gave speeches in practically every American state. She fulfilled her desire for travel, journeying all through Europe. Think about Helen Keller and about yourself. If you had Helen Keller's physical challenges how would you have coped? Would it have stopped you from striving to reach your desired goals? Would you have used your handicap as an excuse for not taking action?

Helen Keller was born a normal child, with sight, speech and hearing intact. The first year of her life was no different from the lives of other babies. All of a sudden, at the tender age of nineteen months, she became seriously ill and lost her eyesight. At first, she was wild, crashing and destroying any object that frustrated her. Her parents did not know how to control her or help her. So, they sent her to the Perkins Institute for the Blind in Boston, Massachusetts. Within one month, her teacher, Anne Sullivan, succeeded in communicating with her. Regarding the moment when she discovered the gift of speech, Helen Keller later wrote in her book, *The Story of My Life*: "It would have been difficult to find a happier child than I was as I lay in my crib at the close of that eventful day and lived over the joys it had brought me, and for the first time, longed for a new day to come."

At the age of twenty, Helen Keller entered Radcliffe College, accompanied by her teacher. By this time, she had regained her power of speech and could read and write. Helen Keller wrote her books and magazine articles using a Braille typewriter. Her sense of touch became extremely important. She had learned to understand what others were saying by placing her fingers lightly over their lips. She enjoyed music by touching the wood of the piano and could even listen to the radio by feeling the vibrations of the radio box. Although she still could not sing, she was able to enjoy vocal music by putting her fingers lightly on the throat of the singer. Helen Keller also had a great memory; she could remember a person she had been introduced to five years earlier merely by the grip of the person's handshake!

Although blindness is horrible enough for many people to think about, Helen Keller claimed that being deaf was an even greater agony. And you think you have problems! Even with all her disadvantages, Helen Keller still garnered the drive to accomplish the goals she set for herself. You may not be physically blind, but are you blind to the need to push yourself in the direction of your goals? You may not be deaf, but are you listening to the inner voice that implores you to reach out for your goals?

Some people let their problems, real or imagined, rob them of the joys of life. They complain on rainy days; they complain on sunny days. And while they find endless ways not to achieve, others are quietly striving to do what it takes to succeed.

If you believe that your lack of education seems to hold you back, go back to school. Does a lack of job skills make you a continual casualty in the job market? Then get the required training. Some use the convenient excuse: "But I am too old!" Refusing to embark on that important journey of discovery of your potential will not bring time to a standstill. One, two, three years later, you might find yourself lamenting why you had not made an effort. It's no fun having to lie on a bed of regret.

With the passing of years, can you honestly say that your time on this planet has been well spent? Only you know the kind of lifestyle you want to design for yourself. No matter what it is, one thing is certain: if you sit on your haunches, there is very little chance that you will be able to attain the personal, financial, emotional, or spiritual freedom that you desire.

Regulate Your Time

Being disciplined, for one thing, means that you know the value of your time. You don't waste your time on unnecessary things. Sure, you have fun. In fact, you should have a lot of fun along the way. Do your goals include making time to enjoy life with your loved ones? Make the most of your time.

Being disciplined means that if, for instance, you want to master programming, you will make the time for it. This may mean lots of solitary moments hunched over the computer, but once you emerge from the cocoon of skill development, you might be ready to take on the world, or at least, have better control over your career direction. Study bootcamps, for example, serve the purpose of providing total immersion and helping people acquire skills within a short time. Have you sought out such an opportunity?

Don't want to be a programmer? Fine. If you desire to be a naturalist, you can't avoid stepping into the woods for frequent first-hand exploration, can you? In any case, use time wisely.

Josh Weston's rule: "39 + 1 > 40 + 0"

Josh Weston is Chairman and Chief Executive Officer of Roseland, New Jersey-based Automated Data Processing, a company with $3.0 billion revenues and 24,000 employees. According to him, it is infinitely more productive to take one hour out of forty to think about one's life and work than to keep rushing headlong week after week working the oft-required 40 hours a week with nary a thought as to whether one is really on the right track or not. Josh Weston's own phenomenal success in the business world gives cause for pause. He knows whereof he speaks when he advises: Take one hour out of 40 for thought and reflection on your life and progress toward your goals.[1]

YOU Make Things Happen

Stop making excuses for yourself. Act. Don't sit around waiting for things to happen. *You* make things happen. Being responsible to yourself means following through on your plan and forcing yourself to move in the direction of your goals.

---

1 Based on telephone interview with Everett Ofori

Be Flexible

Being disciplined does not require that you lock yourself into an inflexible pattern. If your actions are not providing you with the kind of results you need to reach your goal, then change your actions. Do things a little differently, or maybe a lot differently, to get more positive results. Being disciplined means that you never lose sight of your eventual target. Getting there — reaching your dreams — may not be easy, but because you are driven, despite any detours, you will still finally arrive at your goal.

Being disciplined also means being a believer in your own dreams. You may think that success is luck. Sure, some people seem to have all the luck, but if you open your eyes to the different possibilities available to you, learn to recognize opportunity and develop the drive to follow through, your success is also assured.

Being enthusiastic about your aspirations can help you to be disciplined, whether you want to be the next Michael Jordan, Oprah Winfrey, or Bill Gates. If by the time you achieve your goals you've lost all interest in what you set out to do, then you've really just wasted your time. This is why it is important, at the outset, to carefully review your goals and your direction to be sure they are truly what you want. Even if you get it wrong at the beginning, frequent review will allow you to pivot when necessary, to change direction as circumstances demand.

Don't Blame Your Failures on a Witch

For several centuries in Europe, people thought to be witches were hunted down and killed, sometimes through such grotesque methods as burning. Thousands may have died in these witch hunts, and even today, just reading about it can send shivers of disbelief through one's spine. Now, one might suppose that such witch hunts are a relic of the backward past and that in these enlightened times, nothing of the sort could happen.

In some parts of Africa, unfortunately, it is not uncommon to blame every misfortune on the doings of a witch. The death of a child. Check. Failure in an exam. Check. Loss of a job. Check. In such situations, woe betides any elderly lady around whose appearance gives some cause for concern. She must be held responsible!

Blaming a witch for your failure has a double attraction: it excuses you from taking responsibility for your own shortcomings and it exaggerates your sense of importance in your own eyes. After all, if a coven of neighborhood witches are plotting day and night for your downfall, you must be important indeed!

In the article "Why are witches still being burned in Ghana?" noted Ghanaian journalist Cameron Duodu writes:

> *Because belief in witchcraft forms part of Ghanaian mythology, elderly women are often subjected to cruel treatment and mental torture. A lack of scientific knowledge of the natural physical and mental degeneration that can occur during old age -- including Alzheimer's disease, but not excluding hysterical dissociation and schizophrenia -- means that witchcraft is blamed for a lot of "strange" happenings.*

The roadblocks and setbacks that may be standing in the way of your success are not barriers that only you are experiencing because of the nocturnal flying habits of persistent witches. Successful people in or from Australia, Brazil, Chile through Germany, Israel, Yugoslavia, and Zimbabwe can all tell you their own tales of setbacks. They don't blame their problems on the doings of witches. Rather, people succeed by seeking ways to overcome these roadblocks, some of which may be due to the external environment and others due to your own shortcomings. By thinking and strategizing and seeking allies along life's path, you can transcend what may have seemed like a clear case of hindrance orchestrated by a wily, wicked world of witches.

For those in places where it is customary to blame a witch for one's failure, why not focus more attention on the witch within, which has three faces: aversion to facts and knowledge, procrastination, and a tendency to blame others.

You Can Benefit From Associating With A Professional Organization

To sustain you through the difficult times that come your way, you may want to connect with a professional support group. If you've set a professional goal, it might be very worthwhile for you to belong to a professional association. Such an organization can be a great source for resources. Moreover, having a strong network and backbone of experienced people in your field to learn from can help you to weather the disappointments that are sometimes part of a developing career.

Even with a strong drive to keep moving ahead, you could run into a roadblock so severe that you just won't feel like continuing anymore. You may lose all faith in yourself and begin to doubt your own abilities, thinking that others are infinitely better than you and that's why they succeed and you don't.

Remember that even the greatest and most admired people have met with circumstances that seriously challenged their commitment. You can overcome your obstacles if you stand up to them and maintain a positive attitude. There was a time when you believed that you would achieve your goals. Don't let a momentary setback smother the part of you that recognizes your potential to achieve. Don't let the passion you have for your dreams wane.

Remember, when the heat of passion overcomes the calmer reason, one ends up either a fool or a genius! Whip up passion for your talents, persist in your quest, and get ready to share your genius with the world.

DRIVE AND DISCIPLINE - IN A NUTSHELL

* Goethe said, "Whatever you can do, or dream you can, begin it." Set your goals and steadily work toward their accomplishment.

* Drive and self-discipline are the twin engines that will propel you toward completion of your goal.

* Don't let laziness or distractions sink you into mediocrity and oblivion. Take action and develop a forward momentum to meet your aspirations. Act on your thoughts

* Don't allow yourself to be overwhelmed by obstacles. Use Helen Keller as your model.

* Discipline yourself to make the best use of your time.

* Only you can make great things happen - you are responsible for your success.

* Being disciplined does not mean being inflexible; it means keeping your goals in sight at all times.

SELF-DISCIPLINE THROUGH TIME MANAGEMENT

List five ways in which you waste valuable time.

1._____

2._____

3._____

4._____

5._____

Write down the steps you plan to take to make better use of your time while moving in the direction of your goals.

1._____

2._____

3._____

4._____

5._____

Discover The Role Of Self-Esteem

If you tell yourself frequently that you cannot achieve your goals, you won't. You need to give yourself positive messages to achieve. If you don't believe in your goals, nobody else will either.

How secure is your sense of self? Do you have healthy self-esteem? People who lack self-esteem don't pay enough attention to themselves or invest enough in themselves to expand their horizons. They are prone to self-sabotage through indulgence in destructive behaviors. People with low self-esteem may feel incapable of letting their light shine; they may feel that they just do not have what it takes to make a difference in their own lives and in those of others. Getting to the bottom of the problem may mean getting professional help from a psychologist or a counselor in the most relevant field.

Not only do you need a healthy self-esteem to build your confidence, you need to develop a strong ego to succeed.

He who has a why can endure any how.

- Friedrich Nietzsche

6

STRONG EGO

> The "self-image" is the key to human personality and human behavior. Change the self-image and you change the personality and the behavior...
> The development of an adequate, realistic self-image will seem to imbue the individual with new capabilities, new talents and literally turn failure into success.
> - Dr. Maxwell Maltz

If you don't have a strong sense of who you are or what you stand for, you will find it extremely tough to reach your goals. You have to develop the self-assurance to view your goals in a positive light and consider them worthy of your very best efforts. Some people see life only in negative terms. In the company of such a person, if you announced that you wanted to be an astronaut, the first thing he or she would tell you is to be realistic. "Who, you, an astronaut? Take a reality pill."

You would think that with the many examples of individual achievement around, people would grow up with a strong sense of life's possibilities. But this is not necessarily so. There are those who after a whole lifetime, have nothing but stories of woe and broken dreams, the result of the fear and narrowed vision they carried through life. Those who stand firm and never give up on their dreams succeed, in part, because of a strong sense of self and a belief in their dreams.

Back in the 19th century, only the fanciful entertained the idea that humans could make a machine that would defy the pull of gravity and send people soaring like birds into the great blue yonder. Today it is no big news when the space shuttle goes orbiting the earth, when astronauts make repairs in space, or when a robot spacecraft is sent to conduct experiments on Mars. It is very likely that some of those who worked on making the Apollo missions a reality started with a certain measure of disbelief in the idea of sending a manned spacecraft to the moon. But with time and progress, they might have shifted their thought patterns to accommodate what eventually became reality.

The men and women who help make such things possible are those who will not allow their dreams to be dismissed. They are the people who will not be denied the pleasure of seeing their brainchild, their pet projects, their life's work, go from the realm of fancy and fantasy to fact and fulfillment. "What the mind of man can conceive and believe, it can achieve," said Napoleon Hill in his book *Think and Grow Rich*. How true.

Lest you blame your lack of progress on the circumstances of your birth and background, be assured that many of the deprived: the socially and economically disadvantaged, the infirm, and the elderly have been able to transcend their situation to bring some of their dreams to fruition. It certainly is more difficult, the journey can be longer, but it's never impossible.

You Need Supreme Faith

Almost every major discovery or invention was at one time thought impossible. Without supreme faith and the spirit of "can do," we would still be without many of the inventions that are a hallmark of our present civilization. Greatness in any field is hardly ever the result of an accident. What goes on in our minds has a lot to do with whether or not we ever achieve our goals. Certainly, without a strong ego, Abraham Lincoln would have given up on ever having a life in politics long before he became president of the United States. Without a strong ego, the Wright brothers wouldn't have continued trying to invent a flying machine at a time when many people thought the two were lunatics. Nothing great can be accomplished without faith that one's dreams are worthy of one's time and best efforts.

Whether you want to start a business, travel around the world, climb Mount Everest, or invent the ultimate mouse trap, if you let the remarks of others discourage you, you've lost even before you've started. It is a good idea to cultivate a thick hide when you have a powerful dream that you want to see realized. A strong sense of self will sustain you when those around you, wittingly or unwittingly, become brambles of discouragement. A strong sense of self should help you persevere in times of difficulty, simply because you sense an eventual victory - distant as it may seem at times.

Even after you've had the courage to start something you've always wanted to do, without a strong ego you may lose interest or talk yourself out of it. If you have a strong belief in yourself, however, you will invest your vision with positive action and continue to nurture the confidence you need to build your life into one of great achievements. If you have a high sense of self, you see possibility where others see failure; you know you deserve the best, and that you won't get what you deserve by closing yourself off to opportunities.

When you believe you can accomplish something, your mind works overtime to provide you with occasional flashes of brilliance and inspiration -- sparking hope in you that you can indeed achieve. Some of us blunder through a lifetime of lackluster performance and realize at the twilight of life that if we had believed in ourselves things would have worked out much better for us. Unfortunately, by then, we may be thinking that we do not have enough energy or strength to make a meaningful difference in life

Build a strong ego and cultivate self-confidence; it's the perfect way to set yourself up for attracting the best into your life.

Your Unique Perspective

Recognize that you are unique in this universe. There is no one, not even your identical twin, who does everything exactly as you do. Some of your thoughts may be similar to those of others, but the sum of your experiences, perceptions, aptitudes and attitudes will never be exactly the same as those of another person. This should make you stand proud and tall and make you realize that because you are unique, there is a strong likelihood that you can come up with something dramatically different from whatever anybody else believes is possible. Many of us continually condemn and berate ourselves for being inadequate, even when we have all the reasons in the world to pat ourselves on the back.

Why do you consider yourself inadequate? Why do you compare yourself with others? Everyone is different. Erase negative thoughts and feelings from your daily life and let the transforming power of self-confidence take over. But don't be like those who build their self-esteem on high doses of hollow praise rather than on the bedrock of effort and a succession of achievements. Set high expectations for yourself and you will reach them. Your mind has an amazing ability to guide your efforts. Tell yourself you can and you will.

Some people are better skiers than you; others are better dancers; others are better public speakers; others may be better writers, computer programmers, or entertainers. Don't berate yourself because Norman Mailer wrote better novels than you do. Just think how much effort he must have put into developing his craft. Don't put yourself down because you feel you're not as accomplished as others. Instead, use them as positive examples, and take steps to bring yourself up to their level. The good news is that if you put your mind to it, there is nothing in this world that you cannot accomplish.

Georgette Mosbacher - Tap into the force within

Georgette Mosbacher is CEO of an international cosmetics company, Borghese. Mrs. Mosbacher is a glamorous lady. She is a jetsetter, and was once married to the late Robert Mosbacher, former U.S. Secretary of Commerce in George H. Bush's administration. She glories in her success. It's easy to look at the lovely Georgette, her lifestyle and connections and conclude that anyone born beautiful and privileged could attain her current level of success. The truth is that, by her own admission, Georgette didn't have the benefit of either a pretty face or wealthy parents when she was growing up. Rather, it was through force of will and determination, what she calls Feminine Force, that she's come to enjoy her current level of worldly sophistication and success.

For a while Ms. Mosbacher was locked into an abusive relationship with her second husband. It was thanks to her own incredible inner power that she regained her self-esteem, and with that came control of her life. In her book *Feminine Force*, Ms. Mosbacher writes:

> *The Feminine Force is my way of describing the intangible but indelible powers or energies that all women are born with but that many of us lose somewhere along life's way.*
>
> *The Feminine Force operates according to its own principles and moves through each of us. Yet once any part of the Feminine Force is unleashed, it can make the way for all women through the uncharted and unfamiliar terrain of our own possibilities.*

The abuse Georgette suffered at the hands of her second husband took her to one of the lowest points in her life, but she endured. These are her thoughts after one particularly shocking incident of physical abuse:

> *I'd tried to leave him before, but fear of being worthless without him had brought me back every time. In a city where I knew no one else the structure of the life we had together was the only structure I knew, and I needed structure. I felt my only chance was to try to make what I had work; I hadn't had enough life experience to know that being rich and successful and married to a powerful man didn't guarantee your personal fulfillment and self-respect. I hadn't realized that in some cases sacrificing your sense of self was the price you paid.*

Georgette eventually extricated herself from this abusive situation by deciding that she needed to be her own best friend. Today she is far from being a victim, because she took practical steps to regain full control of both her financial life and her relationships.

Because of some of the tactics Ms. Mosbacher used in the past, some have called her a gold digger. She acknowledges some of those earlier errors in her book, *Feminine Force*, but it's important to note that the force that Ms. Mosbacher talks about, while it can be used for good or ill, is not exclusive to women. We may just as well call it Personal Power, Inner Strength, or Inner Force.

Make a pact with yourself. Decide that once and for all you will take charge of your destiny and steel your will toward the achievement of whatever goal you've set for yourself.

Be Yourself or Refashion Yourself?

It is not uncommon to hear the advice "Be Yourself" when one is considering making a change in attitude or approach to life. This assumes that it is somehow deceptive not "to be yourself." But what does it mean to be yourself if you have picked up a lifetime of bad habits that are holding you down? Should you be yourself or should you seek to refashion yourself?

And is it possible for a person to change his or her personality? How can you help yourself if you are a "naturally gloomy" person? Or shall we say, a person not known for being warm or friendly. If this is the case, you probably look on with envy at your outgoing acquaintances who are able to connect with others, attract others into their lives and live as though they were having a ball in life.

If you continued to be yourself, would this not mean more lonely days ahead? Would it be possible to refashion your personality so that you can attract people and opportunity? Like anything, whether you want to have a brighter, more engaging personality, or be better at expressing yourself in public forums, please understand that, when you start down such a new road, you will probably feel uncomfortable, because efforts along the new lines will be totally out of character for you.

After a few weeks or months of effort, however, the happy-looking, positively-attuned version of yourself should begin to seem natural to you and people around you might be disappointed if you returned to your gloomy faced days. On account of your efforts at cheerfulness, people would come to identify you with the sunny disposition and lightheartedness that you want to be known for. Besides, when you consistently hold in your mind a picture of yourself as a happy and contented person, your outward personality will reflect the bright and glorious aspect of your thoughts. So why be yourself if being yourself amounts to expressing a jumble of accumulated habits and behaviours that have not served you well to date?

American social psychologist and Harvard Business School professor, Amy Cuddy, in a TED talk entitled, *Your Body Language Shapes Who You Are,* presents a fascinating account of how we can use power poses to change how we feel, and with that, how the world sees us. More than that, Cuddy's presentation speaks forcefully to the notion of facing our fears rather than retreating into the shadows.

In her own case, as a teenager, she had been involved in an accident, an accident that was so serious that it affected her ability to perform to the same high standard of academic excellence that had defined her life up to that point. For example, she took considerably longer to complete her undergraduate studies because of the effect of the accident. This may also have affected her self-esteem and self-concept because later on in graduate school, when asked to give a twenty-minute presentation, she went into panic mode, explaining to the professor that she simply could not do it.

The professor, undaunted, asked her to embrace the opportunity and to give as many speeches as possible. In effect, rather than running away from what she feared, Cuddy was asked by the professor to face her demons. And she did.

Years later, Cuddy, now working as a professor in one of America's top universities, encountered a student who would not participate in class. When the student explained to Cuddy that she was just not cut out to excel at class participation, Cuddy, now a super confident professor, found herself telling the student: "Of course, you can give great answers in class."

Indeed, that student, in the very next lesson, gave one of the best answers in that class.

The point Cuddy tries to drive home is that even when we feel somewhat inadequate, we can play the role of the position we want to occupy and if we do so long enough, rather than just being a matter of faking it, we would come to embody that ideal image of ourselves and whatever superb performance might be associated with it. In Cuddy's words, "Fake it till you become it!"

It's Okay to Get Help

For some people, low self-esteem can generate a state of depression not so easy to overcome, one that cannot merely be wiped out with a little positive thinking. Some have such a low opinion of themselves and feel so depressed that they feel snuffing out their lives is the only right thing to do. While it takes courage to commit suicide, it takes even more courage to decide to live when things just don't seem to work out. If your self-esteem is suffering so acutely, it would be a very good idea to seek professional help in the form of a psychiatrist or a psychologist. Or else, if you are grounded by a belief in God, the Bible has saved many rudderless men and women from self-destruction. Whether you choose the path of medical or religious intervention, as with anything else, do your homework, and do not let your newfound faith or treatment path become another albatross around your neck.

Can Ego Boosters Rescue You?

While for some people breaking a negative thought pattern is all that is needed to feel worthy again, and to walk through life with a smile and a confident stride, others rely on props to boost their self esteem. Recall how you felt when you wore some exquisitely tailored clothes for the first time? Didn't it raise your self-confidence a notch or two? The same with a new hairdo. Doesn't that make a difference in the way you feel about yourself? With the current obsession about dieting in the Western world, you may find that you may regain some self-confidence with the loss of some pounds. However, if you were to live in some other parts of the world with a more forgiving standard respecting different body types and shapes, you might wish to gain back your weight when you realize how much people pamper and love their heavy mamas! Better, however, not to tie your sense of self-worth with the fluctuations of your weight!

A sense of self should go deeper than mere physical appearance, but new clothes or a new hairdo are simple and easy ways that humans sometimes use to cheer themselves up. This is all right provided it doesn't become an obsession or a compulsion. Taken too far, this is usually seen as an indication that there is a much deeper problem that needs to be addressed. Some people even go to the extent of having plastic surgery to buy back their much needed self-confidence and self-esteem. And it works in certain cases, provided the person realizes that it's just a prop and that overreliance on the surgeon's scalpel can create a whole new set of problems!

Think about this: if former U.S. president Bill Clinton had at some point been dressed in the attire worn by the average New York beggar, would that have made him any less effective in the way he discharged his duties as president of the United States? Perhaps not, because he would still have had the same sharp intellect that made him a Rhodes scholar, law school graduate, governor of Arkansas and later, the president.

Conversely, if you were to pick someone off the streets of New York and give him a wonderful shave, a great haircut, dress him in a presidential suit and put him in a presidential suite, it wouldn't make him any more brilliant, would it? Even if the fellow from the streets had his self-confidence multiplied a hundredfold on account of his new clothes, that alone would not be enough to fit him for the position of the nation's chief executive. However, his new-found confidence may win him a job for which he is qualified, as well as a new awareness of life's possibilities, or even a new love. It is important to remember that if someone doesn't have real substance and ability, then all the props and new clothes in the world won't make a difference.

It's Okay To Be Content

Even if you feel that you may not have achieved very much in your life to date, that shouldn't prevent you from enjoying your current level or status in life. You must begin to believe in and be satisfied with your abilities and rid yourself of the notion that you have to achieve endlessly to be happy. The quest for improvement can exist simultaneously with present-day satisfaction. While striving for more, it's important to realize what you do have and who you are. Remember that success and happiness are not necessarily always linked.

Have you ever seen a four-month-old baby giggling, playing, smiling or just enjoying life? A life of achievement? Not too many infants are accomplished and yet they may enjoy life to the fullest.

If we have to account for every hour, minute, and second before we can rest and be happy, then we'll be miserable indeed. Have you kept an hourly record of all your achievements in life? Some of us have lost years to idleness or plain hard work with no results. Regardless, accept yourself as a unique person worthy of enjoying the best in life. There is power in knowing that even though you are a perfectly worthy person now, you can still transform certain elements in your life for the better.

Leave Perfection To The Heavens

This is not a book of advice urging you to strive for perfection, only for improvement. Not even the greatest of the great men and women in this world have been anything close to perfect. Do your best.

You cannot sit and brood about your imperfections and hope that all will be well some day.

Many well-established institutions, businesses, and careers began as small, shaky enterprises that grew only with time and nurturing.

You've probably heard the oft-quoted Chinese proverb that the journey of a thousand miles starts with a single step. Every step takes you closer to your goal.

NURTURE YOUR EGO

* Remember that having supreme faith and the spirit of "can do" are integral to success. Without them, we would still be without many of the inventions that have become a hallmark of our present civilization.

* Greatness in any field is hardly ever the result of an accident. It takes commitment to an idea, effort, persistence, and a belief that ultimately one's goals will be reached.

* You should first learn to encourage yourself and seek opportunities to demonstrate that you are a person worthy of respect.

* If you are lacking confidence in yourself, you have succumbed to defeat even before the race has begun.

* Developing expertise in a particular field should help build your confidence and sense of self.

* Never forget that as a unique individual there may be something great that only you can offer.

* A strong ego will bind you to your dream so strongly that you cannot allow anyone to keep you from working toward its fulfillment.

* Do you need props to boost your ego, such as exquisitely tailored clothes or a great hairdo?

* Cheerfulness is a winning attitude. It wins you friends and helps you to influence people.

* Don't let the negative remarks of others interfere with your self-confidence and esteem. If you need support, look to those who can give it to you.

* Don't let temporary setbacks prevent you from enjoying life to its fullest. Learn how to be happy and satisfied with your efforts at any given time.

* Take a chance. Many great achievements started as small, shaky enterprises that grew with time and nurturing.

* Remember Professor Amy Cuddy's advice: "Fake it till you become it."

EGO CHECK

Take a moment to reflect on the foregoing points and resolve once and for all to develop and nurture a healthy sense of yourself.

Challenge yourself continually with your goals — begin with little projects and move on to the major ones with which you want to define and characterize your life. You know best what you have to do for yourself. Are you ready? If not, then you may need to educate yourself on the options available to you.

SUCCESS TIPS:

MARJORIE HOLMES, author, columnist; Lake Jackson Hills, Manassas, Virginia, U.S.A. Marjorie Holmes' titles include I've Got to Talk to Somebody, God; Second Wife, Second Life: The Love Story; At Christmas the Heart Goes Home; The Inspirational Writings of Marjorie Holmes: Love and Laughter, Lord, Let Me Love, To Help You Through the Hurting; Gifts Freely Given and Writing Articles from the Heart.

Here are the qualities and character traits that have helped me achieve my goals.

Health, energy, enthusiasm. A burning belief in my own ability, and the determination to succeed...Having a definite goal, and the will to work for it... Patience, persistence, self-discipline. Keeping on schedule. Going to my desk at the same time every day and writing, in spite of other temptations, or whether I even like doing it...A passion for perfection -- rewriting and polishing every word until it was my shining best...Trying not to let any day pass without taking at least a few steps toward my goal.

Luckily, I was a born writer, so my goal was already clear. Knowing writers had to type, I took a course in both typing and shorthand. And by the time I was 14, had learned enough to get me a part-time job in a law office. Which would also enable me to work my way through college. (The only way I could go.)

There I learned to improve my skills while soaking up knowledge; and our assignments were to submit our work to paying markets. While still a sophomore I began to sell a few things, mostly poems. And after that first check for $7.00 for a poem to Weird Tales Magazine, my faith was confirmed. "Now *you're a pro!" our professor cheered, "Go out there and write!"*

As for patience and persistence: Disappointments are inevitable; but successful people pick themselves up and go on. And they never give up on a good idea. It took me 3 years to research and write Two From Galilee and 6 more years to sell it! Yet when finally published it sold literally in the millions, and became one of the 10 best selling novels of the past 25 years. And oh, sweet vindication: when the editors who had turned it down now wooed me with enormous offers for the sequels.

I kept to my schedule even while raising four children (fortunately all born 5 or 6 years apart). They were my first priority, but my work was a close second. I bathed and nursed them all; but the minute they were asleep or at school, I was at my desk. By then I was earning enough to hire someone to do the housework. She needed the work, and I needed her. God wants us to use the talent he gave us as best we can. And if we persist there are rich rewards. For me, a long-running column for the Washington Star. Another for Woman's Day. And hundreds of magazine articles, short stories and poems. As well as thirty-two books. Nine of them novels; the others inspirational, many of them drawn from material in the columns. But the best reward of all is the mail that pours in, from people thanking me for the encouragement, comfort and help all this has been to them. Just knowing that reaching the goal I had set for myself so long ago had actually affected so many lives.

I studied the lives of great men and famous women, and I found that the men and women who got to the top were those who did the jobs they had in hand, with everything they had of energy and enthusiasm and hard work.

- Harry S. Truman

7

EDUCATE YOURSELF TO YOUR OPTIONS IN LIFE

> The true purpose of education is to cherish and unfold the seed of immortality already sown within us; to develop, to their fullest extent, the capacities of every kind with which the God who made us has endowed us.
> - Anna Johnson

It used to be that educators stressed the so-called three R's - Reading, 'Riting and 'Rithmetic as the foundation of education. This is still a good guide to follow for anyone who wishes to increase his or her options. As noted American lawyer Gerry Spence has said, "I believe, as the Native Americans believe, that the greatest gift is the gift of learning, and that that gift is not complete until it is passed on."

With the idea of sharing in mind, self-expression, thus, deserves a lot of attention. No matter how brilliant a person may be, without the ability to communicate either orally or by means of the written word he or she is extremely limited. Regardless of formal education, if you cannot use words to bring your ideas to life, you have at best an unfinished education. Although many highly-accomplished people may have had the benefit of a college education, there are many other successful people who may not necessarily have a college degree. While a college education is no guarantee of success, learning is indispensable for anyone who aspires to success. Even Bill Gates, the poster child often cited by those who are not great fans of university education, has noted for the record:

> *College is perfectly designed for me. I've watched more MIT OpenCourseware than anyone I know. I love taking college courses, love hanging out at college. I didn't leave college because it wasn't suited to me. I left college because I thought I had to move quickly on the Microsoft opportunity. I had already finished three years and if I had used my AP credits properly I would have graduated...I am as fake a dropout as you can get.*[2]

Pursue Knowledge

The pursuit of knowledge need not be a costly undertaking. If you cannot afford the high cost of university education, knowledge can be found in many places and acquired in different ways. It may be as close to you as the used bookshop in your neighborhood. You can start right there. Or get on the Internet and start polishing your mind, by communing with Shakespeare, Einstein, & Co..

Norman Cousins writes in his book *Human Options*: "Nothing in the universe has more grandeur than the infinity of the human mind." He continues: "There can be no civilization without progress, no progress without ideas, no ideas without books."

In spite of the use of television, cassettes, videos, CD-ROMs, radio, and the like, as educational tools, books are still a relatively inexpensive way to acquire knowledge. The habit of reading has lifted more than a few people from the depths of obscurity to, if not fame and fortune, greatness in the satisfaction of having wiped away some of their ignorance. The increasing ubiquity of Internet access and tablet readers such as the Kindle, Nook, Kobo, and the iPad, has created the possibility for students to be exposed to a wider range of knowledge and information than might have been possible through just making periodic visits to the public library.

---

[2] Luisa Kroll, "Bill Gates Says There Is Something Perverse in College Ratings, " *Forbes magazine*, 1/31/2013.

Malcolm X: The Transforming Power of the Word

In his book *The Autobiography of Malcolm X*, Malcolm X writes about his time in prison as a young man. He had to rewrite a letter about 25 times before sending it off to Elijah Muhammad, his spiritual mentor. Not only did he have illegible handwriting, he could hardly make the letter understandable. He came from the streets, where a fast tongue was more of an asset than the ability to push a pen. As a result, his grammar and spelling were atrocious.

But Malcolm X was a man of action and earnestly sought, through reading, to correct the deficiencies in his education.

As he explains in his autobiography,

> *I knew right there in prison that reading had changed forever the course of my life. As I see it today, the ability to read awoke inside me some long dormant craving to be mentally alive. I certainly wasn't seeking any degree, the way a college confers a status symbol upon its students. My homemade education gave me, with every additional book that I read, a little bit more sensitivity to the deafness, dumbness, and blindness that was afflicting the black race in America. Not long ago, an English writer telephoned me from London, asking questions. One was, 'What's your alma mater?' I told him, "Books." ...I could spend the rest of my life reading, just satisfying my curiosity — because you can hardly mention anything that I'm not curious about.*

Malcolm X's formal education ended shortly after the eighth grade, but you would be hard-pressed to call the man uneducated. He addressed members of Harvard University as the invited speaker at Harvard Law School Forum. He spoke to many university student bodies across America, as well as students at the Ibadan University in Nigeria and the University of Ghana, Legon. Malcolm X made radio and television appearances in America and in Africa and was the guest of Saudi Arabian royal dignitaries when he made a pilgrimage to Mecca. His views have lived on because he was able to immortalize himself through his words. His life is a testimony to the importance of self-education and communication.

In 1999, the United States Postal Service issued a commemorative stamp in honor of Malcolm X's life. USPS Governor S. David Fineman noted that Malcolm was selected for this honor because "He was a visionary, a man who dreamed of a better world and dared to do something about it."

Malcolm X recognized his educational deficiencies and did something about the situation. What about you? Should you be reading more?

Profit From The Power Of Knowledge

Throughout history, many who would lead have recognized the necessity of acquiring a good, solid education. The liberating power of education is evident from the lengths tyrants and oppressive regimes often go to prevent others from becoming educated. In the days of slavery in America, slaves were forbidden to learn to read -- dark days indeed for America. Today, in many parts of the world, there is no such proscription against reading except what people impose upon themselves, forgetting that the power and freedom that they seek may be buried in the books that they refuse to read!

In South Africa, when the first tentative steps were made to establish schools for the people in the 18th century, the Afrikaners devised an educational system for the blacks that imparted an attitude of service and subservience to whites. Blacks were not encouraged to pursue intellectual subjects that would lead to such careers as law or the priesthood. Instead, they were taught more "practical" things like cleaning, digging -- using their brawn rather than their brains. It is a comforting thought that as South Africa has closed the book on apartheid, the new sense of freedom includes educational opportunities for all South Africans regardless of color.

If those in power, intent on promoting their own diabolical notions, forbid you to educate yourself, be prepared to fight: Any well-meaning ideology, after all, should be able to withstand the scrutiny of an educated mind.

Gandhi, Nkrumah And L'Amour

Without the benefit of education, Gandhi may not have had the opportunity to communicate his views to the British imperialists and eventually put into action his policy of *satyagraha* or nonviolent resistance. Trained as a lawyer in England, Gandhi had the knowledge to penetrate the thick and unyielding hide of imperialism.

If not for the vision of a few African leaders, many African countries might still be under a cloud of colonial rule. In part, perhaps, these leaders realized that they had a better chance of gaining independence for their people if they could demonstrate to the colonial powers that they were just as capable in their study and application of such subjects as law, economics and government. Efforts of people such as Kwame Nkrumah, who studied in the United States and championed the independence of Ghana from British rule, helped to bring an end to the domination of the continent of Africa by the colonial powers.

Louis L'Amour, the prolific writer of cowboy novels, was self-educated. After leaving school in the tenth grade, he profited greatly from his varied experiences, which included travelling the world while still in his youth. Louis L'Amour had a passion for books and read voraciously.

In his memoir, *Education of a Wandering Man*, L'Amour states: "The idea of education has been so tied to schools, universities, and professors that many assume there is no other way, but education is available to anyone within reach of a library, a post office, or even a newsstand."

One of the more outstanding writers of the 19th century, Mark Twain, did not go to college and it is he who once said: "Training is everything. The peach was once a bitter almond; cauliflower is nothing but cabbage with a college education." Twain also said: "I have never let schooling interfere with my education." Many famous and successful people including Henry James and Harry Truman did not have the benefit of an extensive college education.

Henry David Thoreau, whose works have been studied and dissected by scholars all across the world, claimed that he learned nothing of value at Harvard. One of the most celebrated poets of America, Robert Frost, is said to have given up his Harvard education in disgust. These people did not lose out on education, because they went on to educate themselves. More recently, Bill Gates, founder of Microsoft, left his formal education at Harvard to start a company that has become the world's preeminent computer software development company. When some people find that they are not getting the education they want at university, they leave. Like Frost and Gates, they are lucky if they are motivated enough to continue learning on their own.

Formal schooling is fine if you can afford it, but it is not the *sine qua non* of education; the traditional educational structure is not the only structure by which one can obtain knowledge.

For less than it would cost you to eat in a restaurant, you could buy *History of the World* by J.M. Roberts, *World Religions* by Warren Matthews or National Geographic's *The Science Book: Everything You Need to Know About the World and How it Works*. If you are unable to study formally you still have an obligation to educate yourself. A trip to the bookstore could be the beginning of a lifetime of adventure in expanding your horizons. Some claim that the problem is not a lack of books and opportunity, it's a lack of time.

You Have Time, No?

Think again. Why not make use of all the free time you invariably get riding on buses, waiting for appointments, waiting in various offices. It's a matter of priorities. For some people it is not at all difficult to decide which is more profitable, a few nights of feverish dancing at the clubs or a few nights accumulating knowledge.

Louis L'Amour says of education:

> *It should offer breadth of view, ease of understanding, tolerance for others, and a background from which the mind can explore in any direction. Education should provide the tools for a widening and deepening of life, for increased appreciation of all one sees or experiences. It should equip a person to live life well, to understand what is happening about him, for to live well, one must live with awareness.*

For Louis L'Amour, success meant essentially two things: a comfortable life for his family and the money to purchase books to continue educating himself. You must decide whether book knowledge is what you most need or if something more practical is what you need. No matter what one aspires to be, a measure of education is essential. As well as being a wonderful way to share knowledge on any topic conceivable, books are precious, having played a significant role in advancing civilization. It is important to know that there are many different learning styles and that while one person might do best by seeking knowledge from the pages of books others do better by observing others.

Universities are trying to make higher education accessible to a larger number of people. Some students, however, attend university under pressure from family or friends and are lackadaisical about their own education; but generally those who go to college under the pressure of their own motivation do better and are more likely to get their money's worth from the experience. If you feel you could benefit from a college education, why not take the appropriate steps to enroll in a college near you -- or in a distance learning program.

It is the rare leader who does not have to move his or her followers with words at one time or another. A love for words and a sense of comfort and familiarity with them will certainly do you much good if you aspire to move people, especially in times of crisis. Menachem Begin, for instance, knew the value of reading, even at a very early age. Keep reading!

"Read A Minimum Of One Hundred And Fifty Pages A Day," Says Menachem Begin

In the book *To Win or To Die*, Ned Temko recounts an incident involving a childhood friend of Menachem Begin, Yehuda Rosenman. The two boys were friends and neighbors in the Polish town of Brisk-de-Lita. Yehuda often visited the busy home of the Begins and on one particular day, he found Menachem at home on the couch, reading. Begin was not distracted for a moment from his reading. After waiting awhile to be greeted, Rosenman shouted in disbelief, "Menachem! Why the hell do you ignore me and lie there even though I am sitting here?" Begin laid down his book and responded: "I am going to tell you something you must always remember. It's terribly important for an educated man, if he wants to know things, to read a minimum of a hundred and fifty pages a day."

According to Begin, you must set this as a minimum goal. The material should not be light and entertaining but serious reading and complete concentration is of utmost importance. Making it clear to his younger friend that he didn't mean to be unfriendly, Begin added, "There are always people coming in here. I can't hide myself, because we have a tiny apartment. So I have to make time, to just lie like this and read." Make time? Yes, indeed. Make time.

Menachem Begin, by the way, eventually became prime minister of Israel.

Communicate Effectively; Be A Leader

If you can think well, plan well, speak well, and write well, you have all that you need to change the course of human history -- or at least, your own history.

One of the primary goals of any educational program should be to equip students to communicate well. An inability to articulate thoughts may be a sign of mental laziness or it may be a more deeply-rooted problem. Whatever the case may be, clarity is essential.

There is a definite correlation between greatness and the ability to communicate — great leadership and excellent communication often go hand in hand. Leadership often gravitates to the one who has something worthwhile to share and who can express it. Who is not thrilled to read the immortal phrases that Abraham Lincoln spun at Gettysburg? Who is not moved by John F. Kennedy's rhetoric when he asks passionately, "Ask not what your country can do for you; ask what you can do for your country?" Who does not silently marvel at the elevated speech and thinking of Dr. Martin Luther King, Jr. and his "I Have a Dream" speech?

Besides communicating effectively, it is also essential to be able to marshal facts to support one's position. In a debate, for instance, you will quickly lose ground if you talk in generalities and fail to ask the right questions. Acquire facts and learn to communicate them.

Public Speaking — Are You Prepared?

A discussion of education is incomplete without mentioning public speaking, the most feared experience of all. People cringe at the prospect of addressing a group because they know how humiliating it would be if they were to fail. Fear of failure rears its head once again. There is a reason to be afraid when you are called upon to give a speech — especially on a subject you know nothing about. But it is not without remedy.

Assume for a moment that you are asked to speak for only a few minutes about the role of the Kente cloth in Ashanti culture. You would probably have good reason to panic, because you may not be familiar with the word Kente or what Ashanti stands for. Even if you did, your knowledge may not extend to the deeper historical connection between the two words. But let's say, you do indeed know something about the subject. You may still find it easier to give your speech if the ideas you want to present are somewhat organized. Meditating on your subject can help. Please remember the words of R.S. Lawrence, in the book, *A Guide to Public Speaking: How to Speak Confidently and Convincingly on Every Type of Occasion*: To distinguish yourself as a public speaker of note it is often necessary to think well in private. In other words, make a habit of thinking about things.

Even if your intent is not to develop your speaking skills to the high caliber necessary to work as a trial lawyer, regarding the importance of preparation, you will profit from the observations of Clark Clifford, presented in his book, *Counsel to the President*:

> *For me the key to successful advocacy was and remains preparation -- careful preparation. Even today, when going into court, I rise early the day of my court appearance, and rehearse my presentation as I shave, sometimes going over it again for several hours alone in my bedroom or office. I have seen many good cases lost because they were badly presented.*

In the long run, regardless of whether you are associated with a school or college, to prepare for greatness, it is important to know that it is you, more than anyone else, who is responsible for your education. It is largely up to you. And the paths to a great education, whether through reading, videos, observation, experimentation, are for you to decide.

Learning from Interviews

The Internet, radio, and television, all offer incredible opportunities for entertainment. These media also offer myriad opportunities for education. In the United States, one of the most notable interviewers is Charlie Rose, who brings to his interview table an incredibly wide range of eminent men and women, from actors and architects through scientists and writers to politicians of every shade.

In an interview Charlie Rose conducted with Sir Anthony Hopkins, one of the most acclaimed actors of the contemporary movie scene, Hopkins revealed that as a child he was dysfunctional, hardly fitting in with his classmates. In fact, he was ostracized by his classmates and often called "dummy," hardly an auspicious beginning! But the young Hopkins did not allow the judgment of his mean-spirited classmates to run him aground. In fact, he used the negative vibes from his classmates as fuel to transform himself. As he noted, "The greatest power that was in my life was being the dummy, being ostracized and being relegated to the background in the class...I was always the bottom of the class. It caused a lot of anger." But beyond this, he also began to think, "I will show you!"

An Actor Prepares -- Anthony Hopkins' Secret

Sir Anthony Hopkins, mentioned above, is considered one of the finest practitioners of the acting craft, equally adept on stage and in film roles. A few of the movies in which he has starred, are *Silence of the Lambs*, *The Remains of the Day*, *Slipstream*, and *The Rite*. In one telling moment, Hopkins revealed in an interview with Charlie Rose how well he prepared for each role. In his own words, "I go over the script five hundred times...literally...because I am obsessive." Is it any wonder that Hopkins is considered the consummate actor? Is it any wonder that many people look up to him as the embodiment of acting excellence? Five hundred times!

Matt Damon & Ben Affleck: Actor/Writer Friends

At a very young age, Matt Damon and his friend, Ben Affleck, knew that they wanted to become actors. Rather than just talking about this dream, they took steps towards making their dreams a reality. At a time in life when many teenagers are more concerned about the color of their sneakers or who they want to date, Matt Damon and Ben Affleck were plotting how to get auditions in New York, which was some distance from their Cambridge, Massachusetts home.

Rather than waiting around forever for acting roles to come to them, they also began to consider the idea of writing their own movie scripts. Though Matt Damon knew that he had some writing talent, having been published in *Rolling Stone* at the age of sixteeen, these two young men did not assume that they knew all there was to know about the writing craft. Rather, they asked their agent, Patrick Whitesell, to send them as many movie scripts as he could lay his hands on. As a result, these two friends ended up reading over 200 scripts a year as they sought to write their own masterpieces.

Eventually, they succeeded not only as actors but also as screenwriters, directors, and producers. As Matt Damon told master interviewer Tavis Smiley about the experience of reading so many scripts, "There's so much you learn by osmosis...it's just....they start to make sense to you...people talk about getting your 10,000 hours in...if you work at something you get better at it."

If you are equally interested in becoming a screenwriter, have you been reading two hundred scripts a year? If not, your work is cut out for you.

But...What 10,000 Hours?

British-Canadian journalist Malcolm Gladwell, has staked out an arena in the world of communication as the go-to guy when it comes to bringing interesting but obscure scientific research to the attention of the general public. In his book, *Outliers: The Story of*

Success, Gladwell talks about "The 10,000-hour Rule." This is based on research conducted by neurologist Daniel Levitin, that often the most successful people are also the ones who have spent the most hours at their craft. As Gladwell notes, "Practice isn't the thing you do once you're good. It's the thing you do that makes you good." This gives the impression that beyond the issue of talent, practice makes a big difference.

While some have taken this insight to heart, others criticize Gladwell, wondering if the 10,000-hour figure is correct. Does an actor need 10,000 hours of practice? What about a writer, an engineer, or a scientist? And would someone with absolutely no talent reach the top of the heap merely by putting in 10,000 hours? It is not inconceivable that someone can become a master merely by dint of the hard work of practice but one hopes that a person is spending all these hours practicing a skill, not because of the desire to be better than others, but because the person truly enjoys the pursuit. The young Beatles, the British band, probably did not pull out their clock every jam session, logging how many hours they had spent at practice in an effort to reach 10,000 hours. Neither did scientist Albert Einstein, basketball star Michael Jordan, or gymnast Nadia Comaneci, who got a perfect 10 at the 1976 American Cup at Madison Square Garden.

People who love what they are doing spend a lot of time immersed in it. Losing yourself in a pursuit, day in and day out, has a way of making you good at it. You learn the pitfalls. You make mistakes. You develop ways of overcoming the shortcomings. You develop technical mastery. The subtle ways you manage the technical challenges eventually help you rise to the level of high artistry.

While some see the 10,000 hours as cast in stone, it may be more useful to think of it as a metaphor -- endless practice. As Matt Damon, Ben Affleck, and Sir Anthony Hopkins found out, if you spend so much time doing something, you get good at it. Plain and simple. Hopefully, it is a pursuit that you truly love, not one that has been imposed upon you by someone else.

EDUCATE YOURSELF!

* If you can think well, plan well, speak well, and write well, you have more than you need to change the course of human history -- or at least your own history.
* In the words of Louis L'Amour, education is available to anyone within reach of a library, a post office, or even a newsstand. Teach yourself.

Knowledge Quest

List some practical ways to pursue the knowledge that will advance you toward your goals.

1.

2.

3.

Find and list three books, magazines or journals in your field of interest.

1.

2.

3.

> **All true education is help toward self-discovery and toward self-unfolding.**
>
> - Martin Buber

SUCCESS TIPS:

JOHN C. POLANYI, P.C., C.C., F.R.S. professor, Department of Chemistry, University of Toronto. He was educated at Manchester University, England and was a postdoctoral fellow at Princeton University, U.S.A. and NRC, Canada. He joined the University of Toronto, Canada in 1956. John Polanyi's awards include the 1986 Nobel Prize in Chemistry (shared), the Royal Medal of the Royal Society of London and some thirty honorary degrees from six countries.

Learning is the prime manifestation of the force that keeps us alive. Learning, and the motivation to learn, both stem from a commitment to life.

The rage to know, is surely, part of the initial gift of life. As infants we take incredible risks in the quest for discovery, and very often we take them knowingly. Bruised, bloodied, bawled at, we persist in our experiments into the nature of mass and form.

It would seem, in those early days, that nothing could hold us back from the pursuit of understanding. But, against all expectation, something does. We call it education.

It will not, I hope, come as a surprise to you to learn that my function as a university teacher is bound up as intimately with motivation as with learning. At the tertiary levels of undergraduate and graduate study, there is a tendency for the young to be close to terminally afflicted by education. The need for disciplined study has too often purged them of the desire to reach out, to touch, feel, taste and embrace the world around them, robbing them of the impulse that first impelled them into the world of scholarship. They are so laden with the armour of knowledge that, as is alleged of mediaeval knights, they are in danger of being both invincible and immovable.

It is, I am sad to say, commonplace for advanced students to come to me, part way through their studies, deeply depressed. Discovery is so different from doing the exercises that follow the chapters in a text. In the laboratory a question may admit of no answer within the lifetime of the questioner.

If he but knew it the graduate student has returned to the harsh world of infancy where the problem of shifting the dining room table, or making a leisurely examination of the inside of an electric outlet, can defy solution.

Teachers ought to recall to these young people the joys of discovery that far outweigh the pains.

As teachers we have a powerful means of doing this. The first is a willingness, on our part, to play. Science has its formal trappings. They are indispensable in arriving at new constructs. But beneath these trappings there lies something much more engaging, the naked truth.

Give a child a pile of candies to share out with a friend, and the child will be amazed to find that this can be done successfully with only certain numbers of candies; 2, 4, 6 or 8. A still greater revelation awaits the truly curious. It turns out that certain piles of candies defy the effort to share them equally among any number of people whatsoever (with the exception of one, which is trivial and selfish); not, that is to say, between 2, 3, 4 nor any higher number.

This is reality. In the hands of the professional it becomes the study of prime numbers; 11, 19, 83 and so on...numbers which you will, therefore, seek in vain as solutions to any of the world's multiplication tables.

Why would the Lord construct nature in this fashion? The answer is that she is subtle, and here, lying in our hands, we have a numerical index of that subtlety.

Because, in the universities we are engaged in research, we are in an especially favorable position to pass on to our students a feeling for the source of knowledge, which lies in experience, and not in holy writ.

The teacher at earlier levels, who is often and of necessity dependent on sacred texts bearing the imprint of the relevant ministry, faces a much harder task. He or she needs all the help that we can offer in making contact with the excitement of discovery through experiment or play, while continuing, of course, to uphold a commitment to disciplined enquiry.

All of this would make impossible demands of the educator, were it not for the fact that we are dealing with a process central to our lives. The understanding of it is within us, and the evidence of it is around us.

Through learning we have greatly extended our life-span, and have provided a select group among us with the conveniences of a push-button world. We have had almost half a century to absorb the fact that among the buttons waiting to be pushed are several that could end human history.

Learning presupposes motivation. But equally, motivation stems from learning. The great periods of learning have set civilizations on the march.

It happened in ancient Greece, it happened in the Renaissance, and it is happening once again today in the age of Science. This march has led, twice in my lifetime, to millions being trampled underfoot in pursuit of a fraudulent *scientific utopia; first the genetic purity of the Nazis, and then in the classless society of Marx.*

Meanwhile vast and real changes have been occurring in the power of technology. Weaponry has long-since reached its apotheosis as the ultimate instrument of suicide. The state is seen to be powerless in the face of a new force which, stated shortly, is the truth widely disseminated by modern technology.

Tens of millions in the USSR, in Poland, in Hungary, East Germany, China, South Africa and elsewhere have come to understand this fact. The world's poor, who outnumber all the rest, have only begun to be heard from. Before too long this entire multitude, rich and poor, must, through knowledge and through a sense of common cause, be motivated to save our planet from despoliation.

As never before in history education has become an imperative. It is too feeble a statement to say that education is capable of enriching our lives. It is the very stuff from which our future must be fashioned!

KAZUYOSHI IKEDA, D. Sc., physicist and poet, Osaka, Japan.

I am not only a physicist but also a poet. I was born on July 15, 1928; my birthplace was a fishing village on the coast, which was far from the busy quarters of Fukuoka City. Kyushu University was within ten minutes' walk of my home. Thus I spent my childhood surrounded by both beautiful nature and an academic atmosphere. As a child, I loved the scarlet sun setting over the sea, the colorful shells on the seashore, and the numerous stars in the clear night sky. At the same time, I often saw, with envy and admiration, university students walking near my house with thick books under their arms. These circumstances strongly stimulated me to become in the future a scientist engaged in academic research and a poet singing of the beauties of nature.

As a scientist, I have contributed greatly to theoretical physics, mathematical physics and chemical physics. I have published more than one hundred papers and numerous books. In particular, my papers on the statistical-mechanical theory of the condensation phenomena of gases and the phase transitions in substances, with the full use of my unique original rigorous mathematical method, have been widely noticed and very highly evaluated in the international academic world. In various fields, including these subjects, I have made achievements in theoretical researches on the properties of matter with the application of the statistical mechanics of an assembly of interacting molecules. My interest also extends to the celestial mechanics of comets, and I have theoretically investigated the orbit and motion of the comet whose appearance in 634 and 635 AD. was recorded in the Japanese ancient history "Nihon Syoki".

As a poet, I assert with emphasis that the true poem, essentially different from prose, should have the beauty of rhythm (or metre) as well as the beauty of sentiment. I create many poems of fixed form in the seven-and-five-syllable metre. This metre is the Japanese traditional one in which a line consists of the first part (composed of seven syllables) and the second part (composed of five syllables); it is very beautiful and pleasing to the Japanese people's ears. I compose my poems in both Japanese and English. My English poems are also in the seven-and-five-syllable metre. In my poems I sing of the hearts of many things in nature, and also many artificial things, on the basis of my sincere love for all creation. My poems, full of both lyric emotion and pleasing rhythm, have gained many enthusiastic and admiring readers.

Below are two of my Japanese poems and their English translations by me. Both my Japanese and English poems are in the seven-and-five syllable metre. In the first poem I sing of a tiger who grieves over his own fateful sin of killing and eating his victim and swears to atone for his sin in the next world. The subject of the second poem is a subway or underground train; in it do I find the sadness of civilization, represented by the isolation from the beauty and bounty of nature.

Tora	**A Tiger**
Torite kurawamu Ikimono wo	I will now catch and eat thee, a poor living thing;
Ranran to site nerau nari.	I am staring thee fixedly, my fierce eyes glaring.
Tomoni kanasimi tomoni nake.	In the other world I will compensate thee.
Tika-tetu	**A Subway Train**
Ti no Soko wo yuku Kurogane no	Ah! Thou dost run on the road deep under the ground
Kataki Kuruma yo, na ga ue ni	Thou art an iron carriage of great rigidity.
Teru Hi no Megumi aranaku ni	On thee doth not shine the sun of bounteousness;
Tuki no Urei mo sirazu to yo.	The moon's pathetic beauty hast thou never found.

My sphere of pursuits is very wide. My achievements cover theoretical physics and poetry, and my scientific research ranges from the statistical theory of an assembly of molecules to the mechanical theory of the motion of a comet. Moreover, I have a wide variety of hobbies and interests, including uncommon and rather unique ones: I love seeing Kabuki and Noh plays, seeing and performing Noh farces, chanting Noh songs, reading Japanese classical literature and ancient history, etc., and I have many experiences of appearing on the stage of Noh farces.

In all the fields of interest, however, my goals are essentially the same: The wholehearted pursuit of beauty, whether in the natural world or in the human world, is my lifelong aspiration, supported by my strong religious belief. I firmly believe that the universe was created by God and it originally contains beauty given by the Creator, and that it is mankind's mission to discover, substantiate and polish such beauty. I have, with a sense of mission, been devoting myself to pursuing such beauty through my scientific and poetic work. In the field of theoretical physics and mathematical physics, I have been ardently endeavouring to research into nature by beautiful mathematical arguments based on logical rigour and to find more and more beauty of mathematical orderliness in natural phenomena. In my theoretical-mechanical research on comets, I have scientifically substantiated the ancient people's admiration for the beauty of comets. In the field of poetry, I have been making great efforts to construct a beautiful world consisting of aesthetic feelings and rhythmic words, by employing the traditional metre in the modern poetry.

DR. JOHN HOWARD GIBBONS, government official, physicist; Assistant to the President for Science and Technology and Director of the White House Office of Science and Technology policy, Washington, D.C., U.S.A.. (1993-1998) Dr. Gibbons was charged with providing access to authoritative information and expert scientific, engineering and technological advice for the President, Federal Officials and Congress, and with coordinating science and technology policy throughout the Federal Government of the United States of America.

My formal training in physics, backed by a liberal arts education, enabled me to drink deeply from the sweet spring of basic research for many years. When I took leave from disciplinary research and became immersed in analysis of socio-technical issues, it was a most discomforting step. But having taken it, the new challenges are not only enlivening, but also surprisingly susceptible to the problem-solving approaches I had learned in science.

The lessons:
1) *Training in physics is an effective instrument to learn how to solve many kinds of problems;*
2) *change in professional direction about every decade or so is a great tonic;*
3) *attacking issues from fresh perspectives is a natural ingredient of creativity.*

The only way we can obtain knowledge is through study. Study for most people is like paying taxes or going to the dentist. It is something people do not like to do and something few people will do if it is not absolutely mandatory. Most people believe that graduation day is the end of study....Our libraries and universities are bulging with enough data on every subject to make anyone who is willing to spend the equivalent of one-half hour per night, both intelligent and successful.
    - Dennis Waitley (*Seeds Of Greatness: The Ten Best Kept Secrets of Total Success*)

8

VISUALIZE – AS YOU SEE IT SO IT SHALL BE

A seed that's sown will surely grow
If it be done in faith
And things we 'ven consider low
Were drawn by a unique bait
Heaven's force that did create
Sprang from just one idea
Palpable though ideas are not
They're all we see and touch
The songs and books and films we watch
Are all people's ideas
Can we then say ideas are things?
That surely makes a ring!
 - Everett Ofori

Visualization is the use of the mind to picture certain events or circumstances. These may be circumstances that you would like to see as a reality in your life. Use visualization as one of the weapons in your arsenal to overcome roadblocks and become a winner in life. Visualization gives you a psychological edge by strengthening your desire and building your power of persistence. Do you see the things that you desire as realities even before you attain them?

Better A Thinking Pauper Than A Prince With Half A Brain

You can allow your mind either to impede you or further you. Many people seem to think that if they had been born with all the advantages of royalty, they would be much further along in their journey toward success. No one can deny that having a certain amount of financial cushion is a good thing.

People like Andrew Carnegie, Warren Buffett, Oprah Winfrey, Bill Gates, and Michael Bloomberg are just a few individuals who have contributed a great deal of their wealth towards making the world a better place. You probably intend to do something similar once you have reached the financial success that you seek. Still, advances in the world, whether towards social justice or technological progress, have not necessarily always been the sole preserve of those who were born into wealth. You may occasionally have been shocked to read or hear about the children of wealthy people who are on drugs, in prison, or just plain drifting aimlessly along the highway of life. Your current situation may not be where you want to be or need to be but your clear-eyed awareness of your situation means that, with the kind of effort you are willing to make, there is probably nowhere else to go but up.

Albert Einstein, Isaac Newton, Madame Marie Curie, and Patrick Henry didn't need to be of royal lineage to think their way into the pages of history. In fact, being of a disadvantaged background may sometimes provide a spur that a more comfortable life might not. When you are at the bottom of the totem pole of life you know first-hand just how difficult things can be. You are confronted daily with the harsh realities of a disadvantaged life. If you hate your circumstances badly enough, that in itself could motivate you to try to do something about your situation. Dr. Ben Carson, who made a name for himself as head of pediatric neurosurgery at Johns Hopkins University, speaks of the challenges he faced as a child:

> *We did live in dire poverty. And one of the things I hated was poverty...Some people hate spiders. Some people hate snakes. I hated poverty...I began to read about people of great accomplishment. And*

> *as I read those stories I began to see a connecting thread...I came to understand that I had control of my own destiny. And at that point, I didn't hate poverty anymore, because I knew it was only temporary. I knew I could change that. It was incredibly liberating for me.*

Hardship can motivate. When things are always smooth sailing it is easy to fall into a rut rather than strive to improve yourself. Ease can breed complacency.

No matter how difficult and impossible things seem to be, if you dream often enough about your goals, and take action toward their achievement, you will discover within yourself powers you never knew you had. Don't confine yourself to puny dreams. Dream big: accomplish big.

Power Of Visualization

If you want to be the best race car driver in the world, dreaming about picking apples will not help you fulfill your dream. If you want to be a master orator, you have to see yourself in front of that large crowd, working your magic on them, even down to every inflection of your voice and gestures. Make your dreams vivid and they will come to pass.

In visualizing the things you desire, it is not much help if you create a fuzzy picture. How will you know you've achieved your goal if instead of dreaming of the apple that you want, you visualize a cross between an acorn and an orange? It doesn't work. Define clearly in your mind what you want so that you will know for sure when you have achieved it. If you create a vivid picture of your goal and pursue it, it will be impossible not to reflect success in your life even while you are still on the prowl or in the hunt towards reaching that place of peace or achievement in your life.

You will go a long way before you meet an accomplished person in any field who never imagined himself or herself in a successful position -- years prior to the attainment of the dream. Of course, some people have succeeded way beyond their wildest dreams. They may have dreamed small but won big; imagine what might have come to pass if they had dreamed even bigger.

Aim For Nothing But The Best

Most of us feel no guilt about taking advantage of the best technology to date, whether it's flying in an Airbus or driving a quality car like the Lexus or Mercedes. We cherish well-written books, lose ourselves in well-made movies, plays, or other kinds of performances. If other people had not visualized these things and committed to making them a reality, we would not have the pleasure of enjoying them, would we?

Learn to see with your mind's eye. Create a strong impression of yourself as you would like to be. If you want to be a public speaker of note like Martin Luther King, Jr. or Abraham Lincoln, you can't be passive and leave everything to providence. You have to dream it. You have to practice particular presentations and speeches but also you have to hold on to the image of success you expect of yourself so that when you find yourself in a situation that calls for your oratorical skills, you won't feel out of place.

It helps if you replay in your mind some of your past moments of glory. If you let your mind feed on the positive and memorable moments in your life, the resulting confidence and optimism that this can call up from time to time can assist you as you go through periods of doubt or darkness in your life. It is, perhaps, this kind of visualization that allows American musician, Snoop Lion, formerly known as Snoop Dog, to comment confidently: "I love meeting pressure with performance."

It's important to scrutinize your dreams. Ask yourself what your true needs or wants are. There is no point chasing after a dream when its realization can only bring you misery. Visualize the things you want in full recognition of the kind of lifestyle you want for yourself. Don't nurture any half-baked pictures of your dreams. Be very specific as to your desires and what they mean to you.

So you know what you want. Now start devising a plan that can help you achieve that goal. Yield to your imagination. Think about your situation as often as possible, but not to the point of worrying about it. Anxiety cannot help you achieve your goals; it wastes your energy, leaving you drained. Make a conscious effort to think your challenges through. Think of all the different ways in which you can reach your goals. Make use of any resources that can assist you. Resources, of course, could be knowledge that you gain from mentors, books, acquaintances, friends, family, your own research and observation, or tools, including techniques, money, computers, or otherwise, that can contribute towards the achievement of your goals.

Fill In Knowledge Gaps

An idea may occur to you that appears unfeasible simply because you're not aware of exactly how it can be made to work. There may be a missing link in your knowledge which prevents you from seeing how your idea can come to life. If a lack of information is holding you back from achieving your goals, make it a point to seek it out. It's amazing how soon you can begin to sound like an expert if you devote just a little bit of time every day to finding out about a subject.

Short, Medium, and Long-term Goals

You should have short-term goals, medium-term goals, and long-term goals. This is so difficult for many people to do. Committing their goals to paper is like dragging them to a war they don't want to have anything to do with. But, it's good to remember -- this is a fight for what you deserve. Writing down your goals is both a commitment and a demonstration that your aspirations are important to you. There may be many little goals you must achieve in order to reach your biggest dream. If you write them all out, the path will become much clearer. Writing down your goal, while at the same time maintaining a flexible attitude towards its attainment, gives you a practicable, real-world blueprint for your success.

Are you asking yourself where you want to be six months from now, a year from now, maybe five years from now? You may say that it's not a great idea to visualize yourself ten years from now because it's impossible to know what conditions will be then. Well, nobody knows what the reality will be in ten years, but having an idea of where you want to be also helps you set your sail and point the bow of your ship of dreams in the right direction.

Despite the importance of having goals and projected time frames, the element of flexibility is essential. If for any reason you find yourself achieving a goal a little later than you expected, don't berate yourself. Just keep at it.

Don't get overly worried about being a little late in achieving a certain goal — take it in stride. Instead, pat yourself on the back for your hard work, as long as you are indeed working hard toward those cherished goals! Don't be your own worst enemy. Encourage yourself. Reaching goals is never easy. Think about the feeling of achievement that comes with fulfilling your life-long dreams. It should be exhilarating. Go for your dreams!

Lillian Vernon - A Vision of Unparalleled Success

The name Lillian Vernon was, for over fifty years, one of the most recognized names in the United States. Over 35 million American adults, according to a 1994 Gallup poll, were familiar with the Lillian Vernon name. The Lillian Vernon Corporation was known for promoting gifts, household, gardening, decorative, and children's products through catalogs. In its heyday, the company had in its database the names of more than 15.8 million buyers.

In those days, notable Lillian Vernon customers included Arnold Schwarzenegger, Steven Spielberg, Loretta Lynn, Betty White, Frank Sinatra, Tipper Gore and Hillary Clinton. A few of the awards the founder of the company won over the years include the following: Emory University Legend in Leadership Award, Commendation in the Congressional record, Big Brothers/Big Sisters National Hero Award. A partial listing of the founder's directorships include New York University - Board of Overseers, American Business Conference and Children's Museum of the Arts.

While at the helm of the company, Lillian Vernon was a featured speaker at schools such as Harvard University's Business School, Wharton School and Bryant College.

In 1951, Lillian Vernon was a housewife expecting her first child. She had a dream to get into business and invested her $2000 wedding gift money on a supply of purses and belts. Her first ad, which cost $495 yielded $32,000 in sales and led to what became a company at the forefront of the direct marketing business.

Lillian Vernon harboured a vision of success and worked hard to make it a reality. Carefully consider the advice she shares:

THE ENTREPRENEUR AND THE PROFESSIONAL MANAGER : GETTING THE BEST OF BOTH WORLDS
- by LILLIAN VERNON

Business is certainly a subject close to my heart. Forty three years ago, I was an expectant mother with two thousand dollars to gamble on a new idea. In fiscal year 1994, Lillian Vernon posted sales of over 196.3 million dollars.

I can only marvel at what my doctor never told me about the consequences of pregnancy. Since you are interested in business, I will tell you a bit about how Lillian Vernon grew..and more importantly, why. I'm going to explain my effort to fuse the entrepreneur with the professional manager. Some people say the two cannot mix, but I consider their interaction a marriage made in heaven. Throughout my career, I have learned the importance first of one, then the other...and I try to use the best of both in the Lillian Vernon of today.

...At first, I thought my success was based on luck...the right idea at the right time. I designed a belt and a purse, and monogrammed it with my customer's initials, free of charge. I paid $495 for an ad in Seventeen magazine and received $32,000 in orders in 12 weeks.

This certainly beat my friends' odds at cards, so I tried again with a personalized bookmark...and sales more than doubled. After a while, it happened too often to attribute to mere good fortune.

In 1970, Lillian Vernon posted sales of a million dollars! A million dollars may not seem like a huge amount today, but it was beyond my wildest fantasies when I wrote my original ad. One million was a very respectable volume in 1970.

By the time I hit the million mark, I considered myself more than just lucky. The word "Entrepreneur" was rarely used outside of French class, but that is what I was and what I still am today!

I make quick decisions. I take chances relying on what I consider my golden gut. I try to keep the catalog creative, giving my customers the proverbial offer they can't refuse. And most important, I know everything that is going on. In the early days, it was my only choice....there was nobody else to do the work. During the day, I mailed out the merchandise, and at night, I worked at home doing financial analysis.

Even after the business was established, I seemed to hang on to most of the responsibility.I did all the buying and wrote the catalog copy...tried to do it *all. It worked pretty well for the first half of my career. But things changed after that million dollar year in 1970. I couldn't do it all. Not only was there too little of me to go around, but I was facing a harsh reality. Growing from a million to a multi-million dollar company involved areas such as finance, list management, computers, large-scale fulfillment - realms that were beyond my expertise. To me, M.B.A. meant "Make Better Assessments."*

So I did what needed to be done and did it quickly -- I acted. I tried to cover my shortcomings by surrounding myself with experienced veterans of large corporate cultures, usually from outside the direct marketing industry. There were so few direct marketers in the early 1970's that I filled my ranks with managers from all different walks of life who generally were very savvy to the ways of big business, and they almost killed us.

I don't want to generalize, but some of the executives I hired just couldn't make a decision. They took analysis to the point of paralysis. Every major consideration had to first be studied by a committee.

I hate more than anything to wake up and find that one of my competitors is already doing something that I was planning on. Part of being an entrepreneur is learning from your errors. My mistake was not hiring professional managers. It was letting them work in a non-entrepreneurial fashion. If I've learned anything over the past years, it is the importance of drawing from the best qualities of both the entrepreneur and the professional manager. These are the left and right sides of the business brain, and they must harmonize in a healthy corporation.

Decision making at Lillian Vernon has always been -- and continues to be entrepreneurial. The spirit of the entrepreneur has controlled my major moves. First I decided to launch a catalog when the field was controlled by well-established giants. Secondly, we increased the number of catalogs from two per year to our current 22 editions. We decided to source products from China while Nixon's footprints were still warm from his groundbreaking visit. We built our national distribution center in Virginia Beach in 1988...All of these decisions were made without looking back.

In each case, I got the facts...let them fly...then let it be. I agree with a definition of committee -- a group that takes minutes and wastes hours. How many truly successful committees have you worked on? Committees usually don't provide you with information as much as they insulate you from it. You don't need a weather man to tell you which way the wind is blowing. You do need to gather the important information, act on your best judgment, acknowledge and correct any mistakes.

In direct marketing, thou shall know thy customer is certainly one of the ten commandments for survival. But unlike our competitors, we take a very tactical approach in making their acquaintance. We don't spend thirty thousand dollars on formal market research to predict an item's success. We use space in our catalog to do the same thing.

At the very worst, the item bombs. Yet even then, we only lose a few thousand dollars. At best, we have a popular new item out in the selling arena, while our competitors may still have it in their research files. It's an entrepreneurial approach and one that works. About eighty-nine percent of our items make money.

Lillian Vernon's operating environment is very entrepreneurial. Though our business has multiplied in recent years, I've kept our management team lean. We are probably one of the few organizations our size to operate with a senior staff consisting of a president and fourteen vice presidents. I am available whenever they want to discuss anything, but I leave most of the departmental decisions to them. In the beginning I felt like I was sacrificing my career...but it made sense. I encouraged my staff to act on the good instincts I hired them for and keep me posted on their activities. There's nobody to second-guess their decision or filter information before it reaches my desk. There is nobody to cover up their mistakes. Entrepreneurs must stand or fall on their decisions...and if one of my employees consistently cannot do that, we must part company.

I'm sure this hardly strikes you as a breakthrough in effective management. But think about the number of large corporations that don't operate this way. They shuttle an underperforming employee through several departments. But if Lillian Vernon has marched to the beat of an entrepreneurial heart, I know that it must be tempered by a managerial head if we are to continue to grow. My managers are as important to me as my customer list. They have the expertise I lack. They provide invaluable advice and information. At first, they were a necessity. Now, they are priceless. Thanks to the professional managers, I get informative weekly and monthly reports on every aspect of our business. Using the latest computer technology, our financial and list management experts can pull together data I would never have otherwise imagined to help make better entrepreneurial decisions.

We have frequent strategic planning sessions. This was a great leap forward considering my immediate goal used to be to remain solvent and sane.

Mixing entrepreneurs and managers -- the oil and water of business, is not only possible and profitable, but it's also fun. Both sides learn from the other and grow as individuals. To those of you who are intrigued by or have a professional interest in direct marketing, I'm not being overly optimistic in forecasting a bright future for those who can leverage both entrepreneurial and managerial talents. Our business will continue to grow in the foreseeable future. Our service improves all the time, while it continues to deteriorate in retail stores. In the past three years, retail sales have increased at a much slower annual growth rate than mail order sales.

There is a glut of catalogs currently on the market -- you only have to check your mail to realize how many of us want your business. We are bound to see some direct marketers fall by the wayside -- especially in today's business environment and with the increase in postage rates. The ones who best manage their growth and provide consistent service over a period of time will be around in the long run. Direct mail is so much more competitive than it was when I started with a purse and a dream. These days, we have to approach potential customers with an entire line, a solid marketing plan. And we have to stay on top of a million details...many of which happen after the sale.

Professional management becomes crucial. If an employee misspells the name on a child's coat rack, we better be concerned about it as the child's mother. As soon as we ease up on the details, we will be wondering why our orders disappeared. To those of you in a position to invest or start in a business, give your entrepreneurial spirit a chance. It's one of life's ironies that the more you can prove that you don't need a loan, the better your chances usually are of getting one. This is especially true for start-up businesses.

When I needed money to buy my first major warehouse facility in 1972, my bankers asked about my tangible assets. But my biggest asset, then and now, is intangible. It is my list of some 15.8 million catalog buyers, and it is far more valuable than anything else Lillian Vernon owns. Some bankers were ready to show me the door. They didn't understand that this list, not bricks and mortar, was my guarantee of future profits. Our research shows that customers on our house list buy twice as much merchandise from our catalogs as the average customer on a rental list. In other words, that long list of names translates into very healthy profits on the bottom line.

Lillian Vernon has taught me a lot over the years, but nothing more than good old-fashioned common sense. I try to use common sense in all of my decisions -- perhaps common sense is the core ingredient in the entrepreneur. For years, my friends ask why I am still so involved in merchandising now that the *company is so big. No one can pick a product, approve an Ektachrome, or make a piece of copy sing like a born merchant with good common sense. That is the force behind my catalog -- the common sense way with product, picture and words, and with management!*

So plan your hunches and use your heads and mix in a heavy dose of common sense.

Prepare to Pivot

After a 57-year run of success, Lillian Vernon Corporation was forced to file for bankruptcy protection and eventually sold. How did a company that had been run on common sense principles suddenly find itself gasping for air? The answer, in part, may be -- the Internet.

Lillian Vernon sent colorful catalogs into millions of homes each year. This winning formula had worked for decades, making the company a household name. Once the Internet came on the horizon, many companies continued to operate their businesses as usual and were not quick to realize how they might leverage the power of the Internet to transform their businesses. More nimble, technology-savvy players provided greater convenience than traditional paper-based catalogue marketers. Soon, names like eBay and Yahoo Auction began to dominate, leaving Lillian Vernon and other paper-based catalog marketers in the dust.

So, what is the lesson here? Never stop scanning the environment. Take an interest in new developments and consider how they might affect your business and your life, for good or ill. Those who took an early interest in the Internet have become the new kings and queens of the business world. Though ownership of the company has changed a few times, it seems that finally, Lillian Vernon Corporation has found its Internet feet.

When businesses become so big that they are no longer nimble, it is certain that other more flexible and quicker players will take their place. So, even when you become a giant in your field, don't be the kind of giant whose feet are too heavy -- to dance. Be the kind of person or business that is always prepared to pivot when the need calls for it.

Tell A Few Good Friends

To stick with your dreams and make them a daily focus, announce them to a few key friends, especially those who will give you positive reminders of your commitment. Once you let some people in your life know that you are studying another language, for instance, you make yourself accountable; they are free to ask you how your study of the new language is proceeding. If you value integrity, you will make inroads into satisfying the goal you've set for yourself.

Don't fall into the trap of telling only people who will criticize you and make you feel bad when you are not pulling your weight. Choose people who will be supportive and will encourage you even when things seem tough. Certain people might take delight in making fun of you for being so ambitious, but never mind them; you have to steel yourself against the "attacks" of such people. These are not people you can count on — every achiever has had detractors.

Friends - good friends, that is - can help you clarify your ideas and perhaps contribute some of their own. The kaleidoscope of ideas that can come from your small group of supportive friends can motivate you to reach your goals even faster than if you had to struggle through the details of your plan all by yourself. And while you are enlisting others to help you reach your goals, why not offer yourself as a cheerleader to others who are similarly ambitious?

Your Friends: Do They Have An Identity of Integrity?

If you are going to share your ideas, make sure that it is with people that you truly trust. It is no fun sharing an idea with someone and finding out that the person has beaten you to the punch in implementing the idea. Saddest of all is when the "friend" totally forgets the source of the idea.

You can't go through life mistrustful of everyone you meet, but it is all right to expect a certain level of integrity from those that you want to call your friends.

POINTS TO PONDER

* Learn to see with your mind's eye. Create a strong vivid impression of yourself as you would like to be.

* Visualization is so important that you will go a long way before you meet an accomplished person in any field who never imagined himself or herself to be in their successful position.

* After clarifying your goals on paper or screen, plan the steps you will take to get there. Visualize yourself at various stages along the way. Look for alternative ways to reach your goal(s).

* Never say to yourself that what you want to accomplish has never been done before, so it cannot be done. If you can dream of something and visualize it, there's no reason why you cannot make an attempt to bring it to reality.

* Try to have a few good friends in your corner who can motivate you and give you candid advice. Needless to say, you would do the same for them.

DAILY VISUALIZATION PRACTICE

Many great thoughts and ideas were fashioned in the peaceful environment of solitude. Go to a quiet place and think deeply about your goals. Write down three of the things you see yourself learning or doing in the course of pursuing your major goals. For example, an aspiring politician may visualize herself giving speeches to large audiences complete with great acceptance and applause!

1.

2.

3.

Write down an obstacle or obstacles you may expect to face while pursuing your goal. Now visualize yourself overcoming any such hurdles. Think of concrete ways to get around, under, over, or through your hurdles.

_____

_____

_____

Take some time everyday to think about your goals and how you intend to achieve them. Don't focus too much on the potential roadblocks and let those become the sum of your thoughts. Give your mind over to finding probable solutions. You don't have to set the Great American Goal of writing down fifty pages of what you may want to accomplish. That may be too overwhelming. Learn to do things in little chunks that can be grouped together. If you dwell too heavily on the big picture, you may lose sight of all the little things you need to do to make your big dream happen. Break your goals down and you will find them so much easier to manage.

In any case, have you thought about the value of a mentor?

9

TAP INTO THE MENTAL RESOURCES OF A MENTOR

We are more than half what we are by imitation. The great point, is to choose good models and to study them with care.
- Lord Chesterfield

If you have decided that what you most want to do next year is climb Mount Everest, you have chosen what appears to be a challenging goal. You probably won't break any records since the summit of Mount Everest has been conquered by Sir Edmund Hillary and Sherpa Tenzing Norgay, and numerous others besides. Still, with such a goal, you've given yourself a huge and amazing undertaking. If you decide to follow through with this idea, some factors regarding your trip may demand serious consideration and expert advice. Assuming that you have all the mountain-climbing equipment you need, you'll still need a guide. This person would certainly need to be an expert on the terrain and topography of the area around Mount Everest.

Throughout history, many successful people have found their success by first learning their craft from the hand of a master. Certainly, it is advantageous for a person starting out in some field to learn from a more experienced person something of the techniques that define that particular practice or endeavour. It will profit the individual who wants to stake a claim to fame, fortune, or accomplishment to learn about what has been done before by others in the same subject area. If most of what has been accomplished in the field is at best mediocre, that should give you the impetus to bring a new spirit of excellence into the field. You will find it advantageous to learn something about the lives of people you admire in your field. Newton benefited from standing on the shoulders of giants; so can we.

Regarding those you look up to, it is well worth it to ask: What were the winning elements in their game plan? What were or are their work habits? What about their weaknesses and blindspots? What can you do differently to improve upon what they have done? How can you contribute to humanity by applying your talents as these others might have done? Can you find a pattern among those you study? What sort of things were or are important to them? It's only by asking questions such as these and seeking answers that you can plan not only to duplicate their success but even to surpass it.

Time may be your ally but there are certain opportunities that must be taken while they are red hot. There are also opportunities that may require you to bring others on board in order to accelerate your success. If you decide to go it alone in every case and do things entirely by trial-and-error, your success may be a long time coming. On the other hand, if you model yourself after people who have excelled in your field, you could make wise use of your time by concentrating on the more important things rather than spending precious time learning and relearning what works and what doesn't. Examine the experiences of those who have blazed a similar trail to what you are about to embark on and note what lessons you can learn.

Don't seek to be the carbon copy of someone you admire — you can't. If you do that, you will only end up as a poor imitation. Don't deny your own uniqueness. What you should do is learn principles, habits, values, and qualities that can help you in your own personal quest for excellence. Don't ignore the power of your own mind to sift through what your mentor or role model has to offer you. In fact, many successful people have very well-known foibles and weaknesses; if you seek to emulate every characteristic of someone you admire, you may run yourself aground. Internalize only what you feel will help you.

Be Selective

Take Arthur Erickson, for instance, a brilliant Canadian architect who designed such architectural landmarks as Simon Fraser University in Burnaby, British Columbia. If you were a beginning architect intent on making your mark in the field, you could profit by having someone as bright as Erickson as your mentor. What would you have given for an afternoon of instruction and architectural discussion from this doyen of creativity? Of course, one afternoon would not be enough. Even a year might not be enough for you to pick up all you could from this master architect. But what if you decided that because of his expertise in architecture you would want to imitate him in every respect?

Well, according to Erickson himself, he was far from being a genius when it came to business and financial management. Erickson's company filed for bankruptcy in California largely because of mismanagement and a misplaced belief that a lavish lifestyle would be a good way to attract high rollers who would then contract his services. Many of his employees and associates had no doubt been proud to be associated with him given his creative genius in architecture, but they probably would not have benefited from emulating his management skills or style.

Some of the brightest and best minds throughout history have passed along knowledge for the benefit of future generations. Indeed, some of these people may have done so only for their own ego gratification, not some great humanitarian goal, but since the information is available for public consumption, why not use it?

Whether you aspire to be a preacher, writer, teacher, or scientist, there must be at least one person in your field whose work you admire. Study and dissect the person's life, his or her subject, and learn how that person was able to make things work. Then go and do likewise or modify the techniques you learn to suit your own personality and goals.

None of this advice will do you any good, of course, if you are still not sure about what you want. Nail down your needs and desires in specific terms. That way you can begin to garner all your resources toward the achievement of your goal. How compelling can you be if you are eternally unsure about the things you claim to covet? Knowing exactly what you want is a good foundation for the realization of your dreams. It also helps you determine the kind of mentors and role models you should seek out to assist you.

Make Daily Resolutions

Learn something new and do something positive -- every single day. The little adjustments you make, all the seemingly insignificant things you do that are compatible with your dreams will, in the end, have contributed to the crowning glory of your achievement.

Some people find it useful to make resolutions at the beginning of the year. Excellent, but why don't you let the beginning of every month be a time to reaffirm your goals and redouble your efforts towards their achievement? Why not the beginning of every week? Why not a "To Do" list for every day.

Even celebrations that have no meaning for you may be used successfully to your ends, because they have psychological significance as timemarks; they can be imprinted on your mind as a point in time when you made the commitment to do more and to achieve more.

If it's April Fool's Day, tell yourself how much of a fool you would be if by another April Fool's Day you have done nothing about the things you had planned to do. When we don't keep our goals constantly before us, we lose too easily the passion we need to keep us moving toward their achievement. It's important that every day you do something tangible in the direction of your dreams. Use each event in your life as a catalyst to spur you towards your success. Negative events shouldn't make you look back -- to meet your goals, you can only go forward. In tough times -- be resolute, in times of ease -- plunge ahead. You should awaken each day with your major purpose in life on your mind. That's how great men and women are made!

While you consider your own personal goals, give some thought to larger humanity. Do you see yourself as part of a whole? What are you willing to do to better the human condition or the environmental situation? What legacy do you plan on leaving? What would the world say about you when you make your eventual exit?

POINTS FOR REFLECTION

* Don't forget to nail down your needs, wants, and desires in specific terms so that you can garner all your resources toward their achievement.

* Learn important lessons that have been passed along for the benefit of future generations by some of the best and brightest throughout history.

* Separate your passionate desires from mere wishes and daydreams, so you can seek out the mentors who will be of the greatest benefit to you.

* Learn from others the principles, habits, values, and qualities that can help you in your personal quest for excellence.

* Don't deny your own uniqueness as you seek to learn from others.

* Profit from the vast repository of knowledge in books and other reading materials.

> **One life stamps and influences another, which in turn stamps and influences another, on and on, until the soul of human experience breathes on in generations we'll never even meet.**
> - Mary Kay Blakeley,
> *Wake Me When It's Over* (1988)

THE ROLE MODEL PROGRAM

List three accomplished individuals in your field of interest whose examples you would like to learn from.

1.

2.

3.

a) Find out what sort of personal attributes assisted them in their success.
b) Research what business attributes contributed to their professional success.
c) Find out how you can benefit from membership in a professional association in your field of interest.

Read biographies to learn about lives lived, and learn from both the positive and negative examples. Read articles on skill development, innovation, leadership, inspiration and the like, in newspapers, magazines, newsletters, blogs, and books. Listen to audio or watch videos that highlight achievement, the cultivation of the self, selflessness, and concern for society. These will fuel your passion and help renew your commitment towards what may seem like a never-ending quest at times.

If you have participated in the exercises so far, congratulations. You are right on track. Never quit. Just keep pressing forward and one day, you will be pleasantly surprised to find out that you are squarely within the zone of success you had earlier envisioned.

> **People often say that motivation doesn't last. Well, neither does bathing -- that's why we recommend it daily.**
>
> - Zig Ziglar, American motivational speaker

SUCCESS TIPS:

LIZ ASHTON, president of Camosun College, Victoria, British Columbia, Canada. Dr. Ashton holds a Ph.D. from the University of Texas, an M.Ed.... from OISE, an M.A. from Central Michigan and a BPEd. from the University of Toronto. She is also an accomplished athlete - in 1976, 1980 and 1984, she represented Canada as a member of the Olympic Equestrian team.

I've always been on the forefront of women moving into areas where they hadn't been traditionally.

It's always tough being a pioneer in anything but I had a lot of support from men in the field. My greatest mentors were all men because there were no women mentors. I feel strongly that you need to value people based on their ability to do a job and their competence, not their gender.

I don't like to hear women say 'because I'm a woman, I'm not getting ahead.' Women don't fit the male culture and it's been very difficult for them. You need, as a woman, to be adaptable enough to work with it and not expect (men) to change to suit your style. The reality is, they're going to change, too.[3]

3*As quoted in *Focus on Women*, Victoria, B.C., Canada. (Liz Ashton: The Presidential Suite, April 1995).

DR. SHIRLEY A. R. LEWIS, President of Paine College, Augusta, Georgia, U.S.A. When Dr. Lewis assumed her position on July 1, 1994, she became the first female president of this 112-year-old institution. She has previously worked as a teacher in junior and senior high schools and as a professor in a number of colleges and universities including George Peabody College of Vanderbilt University and Meharry Medical College in Nashville, Tennessee, the University of Pennsylvania in Philadelphia, and Stanford University in Palo Alto, California. Dr. Lewis earned a B.A. degree in Spanish and Speech and Master's of Social Work degree from the University of California at Berkeley. She earned a Ph.D. from Stanford University in language education. Dr. Lewis holds a certificate in African Studies from the Universities of Ghana and London.

My primary source of motivation and support come from my family. As a child, my mother always told me that I could and should succeed. She nurtured me and insisted that I do well in school, even though she anticipated that I would soon surpass her in terms of school knowledge, since she did not pursue college training. My father, on the other hand, who was a college graduate and a high school teacher, taught me my "numbers", word analysis, and music appreciation. My paternal grandmother and my mother both recited poetry to me and played recitation games with me. Thus, although I began life in a coal mining town in West Virginia, and although my parents divorced soon after I was born, I grew up feeling loved, feeling smart and feeling as if I was going places. This is a good start for any child. Since I am Black, and since I began life in a racially segregated environment, these qualities were especially empowering.

Throughout my life, I have found educational achievement to be rewarding. I sought and obtained approval at school for doing well. Making the honor roll was a good thing. Being selected to recite, or write, or run for office was viewed at school and at home as "the right thing."

Church was another powerful source of support for me. Although my mother and I moved to various sites in the United States, we immediately placed ourselves in a church, and I immediately obtained spiritual as well as social support from youth oriented organizations such as the youth choir, youth fellowships, local and national conferences, and speaking engagements.

After much travel, my mother and I settled in Berkeley, California where I attended junior high school through college. The West Coast was, for me, intellectually stimulating and socially intriguing. I appreciated meeting persons from the Asian, Hispanic, Caucasian, Native American and, of course, African American cultures. I think that at an early age, I gained a global perspective.

When I married, my husband and I traveled to the Caribbean, Ghana and other West African countries as well as England and France. Ghana made a lasting impression on us. We studied, made friends, and became permanently attached to West Africa, our original homeland. This experience led to further study of my own cultural origins, achievements of descendants of Africa, and ways in which to impart this wonderful knowledge to others.

Over time, I moved from my first love, teaching in public school, to teaching in college. I worked at the University of California at Berkeley, my alma mater, as a counselor for African American and other Third World students, publisher's assistant at Third World Press in New York, faculty at a number of community colleges, educational researcher at Stanford University where I obtained my doctorate degree and was fund manager for the Black College Fund of the United Methodist Church. In the last position, I was staff to eleven historically Black Colleges and Universities. In this role, I conducted site reviews, developed promotional plans, and managed a fund of over $8 million.

This experience led to my nomination as President of Paine College. After one year in the position, I am delighted and challenged. Paine College has great possibilities, a legacy of achievement, and many students who need a supportive, nurturing, and high-expectations mentor.

My success is a result of my upbringing, positive experiences, and resultant high expectations outlook. My husband's and my daughter, Mendi Dessalines Shirley Lewis, just graduated summa cum laude from Spelman College, having had the same uplifting experience. We are overjoyed that our achievement legacy continues.

DR. JOYCE BROTHERS, television personality, psychologist; Fort Lee, New Jersey, U.S.A. Author of among other books Ten Days to a Successful Memory, The Successful Woman and Positive Plus: The Practical Plan to Liking Yourself Better.

Success to me means enjoying life and giving something back to life. I'm very lucky to have had a long-term marriage of 39 years (before my husband died in 1989), and to know what love is.

I'm also lucky to have a daughter, and son-in-law - both physicians, as well as four lovely grandchildren. Because of my profession I am able to help people and it's a joy to do that.

Two main reasons account for my success:
1) *I am a very hard worker; my daughter calls me Queen of Busy, and*
2) *I'm very conscientious. I've been on the air since 1958 and never once have I been corrected because of getting my facts all mixed up.*

Also, I don't take no for an answer. I'm very determined. Though I've not had any mentors I was influenced by Dr. Margaret Mead who involved herself with the people she studied. I also got myself involved in people's lives starting with my radio career giving advice and teaching people.

To those who feel that because of their gender or minority status their chances for success are slim, my advice is to taste everything on the table, try as many things as possible until you find something that you love to do, something that makes you feel good to wake up to.

The truth is, if you really enjoy what you are doing, you may end up making far more money than someone who gets into a field simply for the sake of money.

Keep trying different things. If you try ten things and one works, good for you; you are ahead of the game. And always remember that success builds on success![4]

---

4 Based on interview with Dr. Joyce Brothers by Everett Ofori.

10

COMMITMENT CAN MAKE ALL THE DIFFERENCE

Commitment is what transforms a promise into reality.
It is the words that speak boldly of your intentions.
And the actions which speak louder than the words.
It is making the time when there is none.
Coming through time after time, year after year after year...
It is the daily triumph of integrity over skepticism.
        - Author unknown

The word COMMITMENT surfaces, perhaps more in the arena of relationships than in the field of goal-setting and achievement. But knowledge of this word in itself doesn't mean much unless one is willing to live by its true meaning. It is said that almost half of all marriages in the United States end in divorce. It's obvious that if you commit foolishly you can damage more than your pocketbook — your whole outlook on life can be soured for a long, long time. The one question that nags at anyone about to make a major commitment is: How do I know that the condition is ripe for me to make this commitment?

People should be forever questioning themselves about the important things in their lives and how much these really mean: careers, relationships or whatever else. While it is true that it is foolish to make a commitment to something lacking a sound foundation, you cannot go on forever studying and observing the object of your desire without ever deciding whether to make a commitment.

If your problem is indecision, then you may need to enlist the help of someone whose judgment you trust.

It's important to note that once you make a commitment, certain doubts and misgivings that you've had will simply dissolve. You may never actually have to face some of the potential difficulties you've envisioned. And for those difficulties that are as real as the rising and setting of the sun, you can work on finding a way to smooth them over or perhaps even eliminate them completely. You have to be committed to win.

Most worthwhile things in life come with a price tag. The price may not be in cold, hard cash, but in time or effort. If you are not committed, you will jump ship at the first sign of rough weather. If you intend to see the fulfillment of your great idea, then you cannot rule out having to face tough times. You cannot cross an ocean without having to encounter some scary-looking waves. Your major commitment will include a certain measure of toil and inconvenience but a committed person accepts the totality of the goal or cause with everything it entails.

Here is the story of a remarkable woman who committed herself to becoming a doctor, and never let up until her goal was achieved.

Dr. Beatrice Engstrand
A Study in Commitment; A Triumph of Determination

Beatrice Engstrand grew up in Massapequa, New York. Even at the tender age of four she knew that to reach her goal of becoming a doctor she had to excel in school.

She maintained a strong academic performance through high school, and at 20 found herself one of the youngest students enrolled in an accelerated medical training program offered by the Medical College of Pennsylvania.

In May 1979, an oral surgeon examining Beatrice discovered a small cyst that the doctors listed as mucoepidermal cancer. Her hard palate had to be taken out and she had to wear a prosthesis to cover the hole the surgeon had made in the roof of her mouth. For the next year she suffered many excruciating headaches and a continually stuffy nose, but she kept at her studies.

One day, in addition to the pain, Beatrice experienced a dimming of her vision. She consulted another doctor who recommended that a biopsy be performed to find whether there was more cancer in the growth area. The biopsy report came out positive.

This meant more operations and the possibility of losing her jaw. Engstrand so badly wanted to be a doctor that, more than the thought of losing part of her face, she feared losing part of her intelligence in the event a brain tumor was diagnosed.

As a preteen Beatrice had been asthmatic; she began to suffer from allergic rhinitis. She lived on antibiotics to help her body fight chronic infections and sore throats. Walking was a major chore.

Even though Beatrice missed many days of school through ill health, her goal of becoming a doctor never dimmed. In her book, *The Gift of Healing*, she explains how her mother helped her keep her dream alive:

> ...my mother never allowed me to become discouraged. I was soon to learn the value of small accomplishments. Each day she insisted that we take a walk. I would lean on her arm for support and we would walk the distance of a telephone pole before I had to go back to bed. Then the following day we would walk the same distance, even further if possible. After six months of this, I managed to walk a quarter of a mile.

> Three times a week, sometimes more often, Mom drove me to Columbia-Presbyterian Babies Hospital for allergy shots. And during those years I saw medicine practiced at its very best - warm, humane, scientific. My health improved under the care of Dr. Andrew Barrett, chairman of the pediatric allergy department at that time, Dr. Bruce Daving, and Dr. Joseph B. Smith. Those three physicians became like an extended family to me. Over and over again during my many visits to their office, I told them that I too was going to become a doctor. At the end of each marking period I looked forward to showing my report card to them. Year after year I brought in report cards filled with A+'s, and I savored their enthusiastic responses to my happy chatter about extracurricular activities.

Beatrice's health woes continued. Another operation was necessary. When finally, it came time to explain what Beatrice's operation would involve, the assistant to the doctor in charge told her, among other things, that he hoped her left eye would be spared! There was no question though that her left upper jaw, gum, teeth, cheekbone, and palate would all be removed. And she was all of 20 years old.

> *That night, waiting for sleep to come, I felt utterly helpless. Before in my life if I wanted to change something about myself -- lose weight, change clothing style -- I could do it. But now my body faced a battle to overcome an illness that threatened life itself. And I lived in that body, it and I inseparable. My mind, intact, remained chained to this body afflicted with this dread illness. Therefore, I too, must face this battle. With God's help, I determined to fight. But it wasn't going to be easy.*

In spite of the unbearable pain after the operation, Beatrice resumed her studies, her mother reading her medical textbooks to her. She received notes and homework at the hospital. She put up a valiant effort to study even as she drifted in and out of consciousness. She was inspired to fight on by her dream of becoming a doctor and of graduating with her class.

The operation was successful in getting rid of the cancer. What remained for her to worry about was the gaping hole in her face stuffed with gauze filling. Speech - was Beatrice's next challenge. Thanks to a ventriloquism technique she had learned as a child she began to communicate, not clearly, but definitely a start in the right direction.

Her mother continued to reassure her that her appearance was improving constantly. To keep her own spirits up Engstrand's mother read the Bible, Norman Cousin's *Anatomy of an Illness*, and other inspirational books and articles. Shortly after the surgery, Beatrice was released from the hospital to go see a prosthodontist. The taxi driver who took her, eager to offer his sympathies, blurted out: "Oh, I'm sorry you were hit by a Mack truck!" Beatrice continues:

> *On my first trip to the prosthodontist, he couldn't put an impression in. My mouth wouldn't open the width of one*

finger. He gave me a pyramid-shaped crowbar with grooves. I was to insert this into my mouth, twist it, and try to crank my mouth open for six hours a day for many months that year. I had to get to use my mouth and face muscles again so that I could open my mouth wide enough to be worked on. I got the device that day and practiced with it from then on.

Three weeks after having the operation, Beatrice was back in school taking medical school examinations orally. Fortunately, when she had to take written exams she was permitted extra time. In order to catch up with missed courses she gave up subsequent vacations to concentrate on her studies.

In spite of her prosthesis Beatrice volunteered one day to prepare a speech on geriatrics. Her presentation so gripped the audience that after the speech she received a standing ovation.

Beatrice Engstrand also used the power of imaging or visualization to help her through her ordeal. She believed that the mind has the power to shape one's body and one's world. As she tells it, on May 30, 1984,

...alongside my fellow six-year students from Lehigh, I received the M.D. degree from the Medical College of Pennsylvania. On Founders' Day I was completely surprised and thrilled when Dean Shoeman presented me with 2 awards: The Beatrice Sterling Hollander, M.D. WMC '41 Memorial Prize to the student in the graduating class who shows promise of leadership, high character and creativity in her profession; and the Leopold Canales award for excellence in neurology. I also graduated as a Humanities Scholar, and I had matched at North Shore University Hospital, Manhasset, New York, for internship at the New York Hospital - Cornell University Medical Center in Manhattan for neurology residency.

Beatrice Engstrand had many opportunities to bail out of her commitment to becoming a doctor. But of course, she stuck with her goal, classic proof of what is possible when one makes a date with destiny and commits to a goal. Truly, a triumph of determination worthy of emulation.

Nelson Mandela Knows The Meaning Of Commitment

At a very early age, Nelson Mandela committed himself to the cause of justice in South Africa and as a result, spent 27 years in jail. Having to spend the best years of one's life behind bars would break the spirit of many a waffling man or woman. Mandela was committed to a goal and every price he had to pay to achieve that goal was worth it because the commitment came first.

When Mandela was released from prison in 1990, did he rush off to make up for the lost years, perhaps renting a cabin in a Balinese hideaway? No, rather he continued from where he had left off, negotiating, talking and hammering out deals that eventually paved the way for a one person, one vote election in South Africa. Along with F.W. de Klerk, he won the Nobel Peace prize for taking a conciliatory stance and promoting the view of a new South Africa in which there would be racial harmony and equality among all the different racial and population groups.

Mandela, once branded a terrorist by the ruling white minority government, emerged victorious for his commitment when he was inaugurated president of South Africa on May 10th, 1994, following a general election which allowed blacks to vote for the first time in the nation's history.

Many people struggle for a lifetime so that they can relax in their retirement years. These people understand that it is not wasteful to commit twenty, thirty or even forty years of their life to something they care about - ease in their later years when they may have neither the strength nor the inclination to be committed to anything strenuous.

You can't go about expecting that everything you tackle in life will be easy.

Learning to be a pilot has its hairy moments. If you gave up at the first encounter of turbulence, you might as well say goodbye to the dream you've been nurturing for so long.

Learning to be a writer is like walking on slippery ground and many a best-selling author knows exactly what the word frustration means. If you want to be a preacher you know how much apathy there is among people who no longer have any respect for the standards of the Bible that you may be upholding. If you want to start your own business, you had better prepare yourself to meet the many challenges and difficulties that this responsibility entails.

When you begin anything new, your ignorance may be likened to a darkness, which gradually fades into the morning of a knowledge-filled day. You've got to be committed to see success. At the first sign of trouble you may wonder how in the world you ever came to the decision to pursue what seems an impossible-seeming dream. You may chalk it all up to a big, bad mistake you never want to repeat — but have you given yourself enough time to get over the initial aggravations?

If you are committed, you will work on building your courage and develop the power of perseverance you need to see your dreams through to completion. Once you commit yourself to a goal, you both clarify and simplify your life. You can focus your full attention on what is really important to you. And there is nothing wrong with asking for the assistance of more knowledgeable people before you make a commitment. So-called experts do it all the time. Before some companies commit to a project they hold a meeting, sometimes several, where all those involved in the project brainstorm to determine whether it is worth committing dollars, time, and energy to it. Why not you? Seek advice when necessary.

Mark McCormack Committed Himself To Quality

Mark H. McCormack founded a company in the early 1960s that gave birth to an industry. With $500, he started his company, in what is now called the sports management and sports marketing industry. Today, this company, International Management Group (IMG), not only has a string of offices around the globe but makes several hundred million dollars in revenue every year.

McCormack started out as a young attorney looking for a way to merge his lifelong passion for golf with his everyday business activities. He was smart enough to realize that it makes good business sense if you can make a living at something you feel very passionate about — it would seem less like work and more like play.

He qualified for the 1958 U.S. Open. What happened then to his dreams of being the number-one golf player in the world? Well, if he had trained harder and longer he might have achieved this goal, but who knows? McCormack knew better than to think that he was headed for the Golf Hall of Fame. Instead, he had a bright idea — to represent those who would make it big on the professional golf tour circuit.

McCormack credits some of his success to common sense, but is also quick to point out that he made an early commitment to quality which stood him in such good stead that in one year his company grossed $200,000,000. Not bad. He committed himself to representing only the best, both in terms of their success as golf players and their character. He wanted to be proud of his associations and to ensure that they were ones that would not hurt him personally or professionally.

Did McCormack know all about sports management when he started? He knew about golf and sports and learned management skills both from his Harvard university business education and through personal experience. Notwithstanding his knowledge, had he not made that early commitment, his life might have taken another turn. McCormack might still have been a successful lawyer financially but the question is: Would he have been as happy?

Making the right commitment has a payoff in creating the opportunity to learn many new skills. As every successful entrepreneur knows, one has to be willing to bear the initial insecurities, such as having neither a steady income nor any guarantees of success. Many people who start their own businesses start with what seem like inflated figures -- they think they will be wildly successful and make a million dollars in six weeks. Although it certainly is not outside the realm of possibility, most often, not only does it take longer to make that magic million dollars, but there is much to learn and many obstacles to face along the way.

Sometimes, once you have an idea, you may not be able to determine whether it's a winning one until you've tested it in the marketplace by setting up and hanging your shingle, which today, could mean having a website or a brick-and-mortar facility. Before long, you will know whether or not you have a winner on your hands. Don't analyze your new business idea to a premature death. Some people are in the habit of looking at only the negative aspects of things. You may casually mention a new business idea you have to someone and before you are ready for it, the person is assaulting the idea from every angle, tearing it apart and telling you all the reasons why it will not succeed. It is definitely a good idea to go over all the pros and cons of a project but if you do not believe in your idea strongly enough, you will give up before you have given it a try. Entrepreneurs see visions all the time. If all the inventors, entrepreneurs, writers and the like had listened to all the advice they got from well-meaning "experts," we may never have had the airplane, Disneyland, or many of the great works of literature that were once the product of the imaginations of people who believed in their own ideas enough to carry them through.

**Bill Cosby's Commitment To A Dream
Was Two Volkswagens And A $39,000 Home**

Bill Cosby is known to millions around the world as the funny-man millionaire who has also made inroads into the literary world as an author of books including *Childhood* and *Love and Marriage.*

When Cosby was growing up, he nurtured a fantasy life of someday earning $365 dollars a week and owning two Volkswagens and a $39,000 house. Within three months of working as a comedian, he surpassed this financial vision.

Cosby was a Temple University student who so badly wanted to be a comedian that he left school to concentrate on his dream. He committed himself to getting this career going. Cosby's success attests to the power inherent in making a commitment to a dream.

Having always wanted a formal education, when he left school to pursue his career, he looked at it as a postponement rather than a resignation. While doing his comedy routines around the country he had many great learning experiences. He did go back to school, eventually obtaining a Ph.D in education. His commitment to his dream obviously paid off in more ways than one.

Cosby has turned out to be one of the most generous philanthropists in America.

Make Time For Practice

Whether you want to be a comedian, writer, technician, entrepreneur, lawyer, professional basketball player, a movie star or something else, there may be times in your life when you wrestle mentally to figure out how much time you should devote to this dream of yours. Those who have the daring to reach out wholeheartedly for their dreams are those who profit in the end. Make no mistake about it: if you want to achieve your goals, you must abandon any halfheartedness. Completely commit yourself to your goal and watch things work in your favour. Accept that with commitment comes the responsibility of making the time to develop skills that will take you further along in the direction of your dreams.

A person making a comfortable living as a sales representative may have little incentive to give up this job to become the comedian that he so dearly wants to be. If our friend the sales rep doesn't make the commitment to one or the other of these professions, he may be cheating himself because while doing his sales job all he does is dream about what could have been. He dissipates his energies daydreaming and does nothing fruitful about his desire to be a comedian. His career in sales may suffer and his dream of being a comedian never leaves the realm of fantasy.

For this salesman, it is no doubt a risky proposition to leave his secure job and face possible failure as a comedian. He may remain a frustrated salesman, hogtied to his paycheck, and unable to commit to being a comedian. However, once he commits to being a comedian he will make room for his dream by finding a way to support himself that will not encroach on his need to develop his comedic talents. It may even mean hanging on to the sales job on a part-time basis.

If this aspiring comedian is wise, he will use every opportunity to practice. By the time he is ready to go on the club circuit, he won't be completely naive about the world he is entering. He will probably have spent many a night in the clubs listening to other people and studying their techniques. He may have read a few books regarding his interest and perhaps got himself a few bookings here and there. He might even get to appreciate that for most comedians, the path to glory is not necessarily a straight one.

The initial preparation stage is crucial in practically every field of endeavor. Take writing for example. For certain writers, just making the time to write is a great challenge. The demands of work, family, and real or imagined duties may make it next to impossible to squeeze out a single decent sentence. Truly ambitious writers, however, have been known to use moments such as their coffee breaks at work or a night of insomnia to their advantage. These stolen hours or minutes have even yielded publishable works.

If you are committed to being the best actor you can be, you may find that it is not profitable to spend all your hours sleeping. Would more attention to the theory and practice of the art not better serve your goals? While it's important to build time into our lives for relaxation, you may also find yourself engaging in activities that are not only unproductive but even debilitating to your capacity to achieve your goal. Reflect on your purpose in life and if you are committed enough, you will find a way to push aside those activities that only serve to distract you from your main goal. You have to decide whether it is more profitable to party every night or to use some of that time to advance yourself in the direction of your goals.

If You Go It Alone You Have A Long Way To Go

Michael Jackson has been listed in the *Guinness Book of World Records* as having sold more copies of one album than any other musician in history — his Thriller album. A very talented fellow, he was in the music business at a very early age -- five! Once his career became established, despite his prodigious talents, he did not do everything by himself. No, Michael Jackson was not his own lawyer, secretary, producer, or publicist. He used the services of other people so that he could devote his attention to the things he did best: singing, dancing, and giving money to the causes he believed in.

The acknowledgment pages of books provide a wealth of untapped wisdom. These pages are often full of delightful surprises. Even some of the best writers sometimes have more than one editor to thank for making sense of their work and polishing it for the benefit of the reading public. Some of the best scientists may have a number of equally brilliant colleagues to thank for helping with ideas. It is not always wise to go it entirely alone — not even in a craft as solitary as fiction writing where the writer has to cudgel his or her brains to come up with a good story. Some writers have as best friends librarians in libraries great and small around the world. So, the ring of truth in their works may be due as much to their own talents as writers as to the well-cultivated friendships they have with people who know how to burrow into obscure stacks in library basements.

Preparation Yields Multiple Benefits

The preparation that follows one's commitment to a cause often pays off in developing skills that are important in other areas of life. In the course of starting and running a business, for example, you may also learn to manage people, raise money, keep track of inventory and learn a whole host of other skills. And there is always the chance that you will actually succeed, in which case you'll need certain skills to deal with your success. Even if things don't work out as well as you would like, you can live with the satisfaction of having tried and failed, rather than not having tried at all. As Napoleon Hill said, "Every adversity carries with it the seed of an equivalent or greater benefit."

What you may look upon as failure may be a setback indeed, but if you look carefully enough there may be a positive aspect to it; at the very least, you would have learned many new things that you could now apply to another attempt.

THE FINAL COMMITMENT

If you were to commit yourself to a single major purpose in life around which everything else revolves, what would it be?

_____

_____

Great! Congratulations if you've been able to narrow down your goals to a single major purpose. It does not mean that you will have to forget about all the other things you want to accomplish. This just makes you put first things first. As a reminder, there's a price to pay to achieve this great goal of yours.

11

ARE YOU WILLING TO PAY THE PRICE AND SACRIFICE?

Was anything real ever gained without sacrifice of some kind?

- Arthur Helps

In this age of instant gratification it may sound gauche to talk about sacrifice. But as any successful person knows, if you have all the ingredients to success yet remain unwilling to make sacrifices in your life, your chances of success are greatly diminished.

If you choose to go to medical school, for instance, it may mean not only shelving your other dream of being an active socialite, but also embracing the reality of having to go through grueling training before you earn the coveted title of M.D..

If your dream is not consuming you to the point where you think about it first thing when you wake up and last thing before you retire, you may find it a bit tough to make the kind of sacrifices you need to make it happen. Your dream has to be extremely important to you for it to be worthy of the sacrifices you may have to make in your life. If not, at the first hint of trouble you will pack it in and seek a more comfortable existence.

One of the sacrifices you may have to live with as you struggle to make your dreams come true might be financial. Many people in creative fields such as music, writing and art know financial strife full well. Are you willing to sacrifice the opportunity for a higher income to nurse and develop your dreams?

If you can answer affirmatively, and back it up in fact, you are going in the right direction. If not, it's time to reassess how much your dreams really mean to you. In fairness, being committed to a lofty dream does not mean having to make a vow of poverty. If you can find a job that leaves room for you to pursue your passion, all power to you. Hold on to it. Many have had to juggle opportunities for a while until the road was clear for a single-minded pursuit.

Time should be of primary concern to you. We all have 24 hours a day within which to work and play, yet some people seem to get more out of their time than others. Eliminate activities that waste time.

If you want to live long enough to enjoy the fruits of your toil, do not neglect your health. Take into consideration that a few minutes of exercise a day is a very wise use of your time. In fact, it's hardly a sacrifice since it can contribute to your longevity and eventual success. Of course, unless you aspire to be a fitness guru, you would have to keep your exercise regimen in proper perspective, so you don't make it the whole focus of your life.

Today, there is no shortage of activities clamoring for our attention: restaurants and museums to visit, travelling to do, books to read, operas to see, symphonies to attend, video games to play, courses to take, cruises to go on, and videos and television shows to watch. Some of these can be enjoyable and relaxing, but be careful that you do not allow over-indulgence in any of these pastimes to rob you of time that you could devote to your major purpose or goal in life.

Be conscious of time and ration it wisely. You can't just sit down and wait for things to fall into your lap. You have to take action. If you are a painter, you don't succeed in holding an exhibition when you have nothing to show. Have a project on hand. What is your current project? What are you doing to advance in the direction of your goals? At the same time, you want to keep the kind of balance that assures that you are enjoying the present while still working to achieve your overarching goals and purpose in life.

People who live with other family members have to make a beautiful balancing work on creating a fine balance. You cannot live in a family home and remain aloof. You need to tend to your own needs as well as those of other family members. In some cases, family members may have to make sacrifices of their own to cut down on the demands they make on one another's time. There is nothing better than spending time with loved ones, but if you prevent your loved ones from fulfilling their dreams by appropriating all their time, you are not doing them any favors. It all boils down to the importance of allotting time for certain things and knowing what time is yours as an individual and what belongs to the family as a unit.

Some married people lament how much they wish they had postponed marriage to achieve certain goals. They envy single people their freedom, even as some single people are desperately looking for conjugal bliss. Whether married or single, it seems that what is important is the level of control one has over one's time.

Don't view those around you, though, as "enemies" preventing you from achieving your goals. There are many ways family members support one another and you cannot be oblivious to such blessings that may already exist in your life.

Where There Is A Will

Use every event in your life to renew your commitment to your dreams and goals, thereby keeping them forever before your eyes. Build courage to overcome your fears, learn the value of "stick-to-it-iveness," develop your talents, drive yourself in the direction of your goals, nurture your ego and maintain a strong sense of your unique position in this world. Educate yourself through apprenticeships, reading, courses, or whatever means are available and useful to your own particular goals. Visualize yourself as having already achieved your goal. Model yourself after successful people in your field, but remember not to put anyone on a pedestal. You don't want to have to shelve your own dreams because someone you've chosen to put on a pedestal has fallen from that perch.

Mother Teresa Spread Compassion

Rumor had it that Mother Teresa travelled around the world without a passport, that, she was so well known around the world that only a novice customs official would commit the *faux pas* of inspecting her passport or baggage. Apocryphal though this might be, it reflects what a legendary figure Mother Teresa was in her lifetime.

Mother Teresa was not a latter-day Houdini. She neither walked on water nor brought economic sanity back to some country tottering on the brink of collapse. She did not raise people from the dead. But from Bombay in India to the heart of New York city, U.S.A., Mother Teresa and her army of sisters of the Missionaries of Charity taught the world through their example of selflessness what it means to care for the dejected, the distressed, the diseased, and the dying.

Background of the Saint

Mother Teresa was born Agnes Bojaxhiu, the daughter of a prosperous merchant in the Albanian town of Skopje. She entered the Irish order of Loreto at the age of eighteen and took the name Teresa, which to her, signified humility.

For sixteen years after her January 6, 1929, arrival in Calcutta, India, she taught geography to the daughters of rich Bengali families.

The great turning point in Mother Teresa's life was 1946. On a trip for a retreat to Darjeeling at the foothills of the Himalayas she felt in her heart a command from Christ Jesus to leave the comfortable surroundings of her convent and dedicate herself to serving the needs of the dispossessed, the damned, the condemned.

While her superiors at the convent worried about Mother Teresa's state of mind, the young woman wrote a letter to Rome seeking the consent of the Holy Father to start her charitable work. After a two-year wait she got the needed permission.

In a few years, Mother Teresa outgrew the squeamish young lady she had been when she had first started tending to the wounds of the sick. Though committed to a life of poverty, she was rich in faith and good works, and like the other members of the Missionaries of Charity, committed to whole-souled free service to the poorest of the poor.

Was Mother Teresa a success? The results of her efforts are there for all to see. Was she fulfilled? Having found her purpose in life, she must have been, as she continued throughout her life to win friends among the dying men and women who found in their lonely last days some comfort in the thought that, thanks to the caring hands of these courageous sisters, the world was not altogether a cold and uncaring place.

Mother Teresa spread her gift of love and compassion to the farthest reaches of the earth. In Melbourne, Rome, Detroit, Marseilles, Rio, Chicago, Los Angeles, and New York she set up havens for the destitute.

Mother Teresa's success as an international caregiver is proof positive that it is not only in the boardrooms, the laboratories, and ivory towers that people can find fulfillment and purpose for their lives. Life is rich - with options for personal fulfillment.

Listen to the still small voice...of your heart - and mind. From what you hear...you may find yourself at the beginning of the greatest personal adventure of your life.

Three African Nobel Laureates
1) Professor Wangari Maathai -- *Mottainai*

The late Professor Wangari Maathai is a shining example of what one person, in connection with others, can achieve. Her ideas, works, and dreams live through those that she was able to touch with her passion, knowledge, and wisdom. Rather than just complaining about conditions in her country, Kenya, and other parts of Africa, Professor Maathai recognized that she and millions of Africans had a sense of agency and that they could do something about the sense of urgency surrounding the environment and the health of the planet.

Professor Maathai borrowed a concept from another part of the world to help drive home the importance of protecting our planet. As she noted in a keynote address during the Second World Congress of Agroforestry, "allow me to introduce to you a Japanese concept known as *Mottainai*, which embraces not only the 3Rs, but also urges respect, gratitude and utilization of resources without wasting or overconsuming. The *Mottainai* concept is embedded in Japanese tradition and faith based practices." This passion for sharing ideas about how we can protect the environment, not as something that others must do, but as something that we can all participate in, contributed to her recognition as a Nobel laureate in 2004.

In her Nobel address, Professor Maathai paid tribute to the thousands of people and groups that had worked with her. She shared her childhood experience of watching forests slashed and burned with no thought for the future, and she reminded us that wisdom is all around us and that, sometimes, all we need to do is look within or engage those around us to find a better path. As she noted,

> *In 1977, when we started the Green Belt Movement, I was partly responding to needs identified by rural women, namely lack of firewood, clean drinking water, balanced diets, shelter and income.... Tree planting became a natural choice to address some of the initial basic needs identified by women. Also, tree planting is simple, attainable and guarantees quick, successful results within a reasonable amount of time.*

Though the environmental degradation that Professor Maathai was fighting continues, she sowed seeds of concern in the hearts of numerous people, meaning that the forces of degradation need not hold sway because they can be met with the force of moral and practical action, a challenge that each new generation will have to take up if this earth is to survive. Professor Maathai did not focus on what she lacked; she looked to what she had -- the people around her, their wisdom, and the need to take action.

2) Leymah Gbowee: Tapping into the Power Within

Liberia, a small country in West Africa, the home of returned slaves from America, and for many years a haven of peace, became in the 1990s a veritable hellhole of atrocities.

When Charles Taylor became the president of Liberia in 1997, there were high hopes that he would help the country move forward from years of stagnation and discord. Taylor, unfortunately, drove the country deeper into a moral mess by supplying arms to neighboring Sierra Leone in exchange for diamonds. Detractors of Taylor sought to overthrow him, throwing the country into a civil war that left a river of blood and tears in its wake. In the midst of this mayhem, one woman emerged a leader, working alongside thousands of other Liberian women, Christian, Muslim, and otherwise, all of whom sought to reclaim their country from the ravages of war.

This struggle, which united the women of Liberia, and eventually led to the signing of a peace accord and the arrest of Charles Taylor, is detailed in Gbowee's book, *Mighty Be Our Powers: How Sisterhood, Prayer and Sex Changed a Nation at War*.

Rather than taking up arms, Gbowee and her sisters wore white, literally, and stood together to demand peace. The Nobel Peace Prize that she won has allowed her to continue spreading her message of hope and empowerment to the farthest reaches of the earth.

3) Ellen Johnson Sirleaf: Africa's First Female President

When peace finally came to Liberia in 2003, one of the individuals who was ready to serve the needs of the people was Johnson Sirleaf. She had served in an earlier government, and was not unfamiliar with the corridors of power. She had also run in the 1997 election, in which she lost to Charles Taylor.

Johnson Sirleaf, an economist with a Master's degree in Public Administration from Harvard University, stepped in to try again to serve the political needs of her people. She won her first presidential election in 2005 and won a second term in 2011. Her efforts in rebuilding her shattered country and in giving hope to millions of people in Africa and elsewhere were rewarded with a Nobel Prize in 2011, which was presented to her alongside two other remarkable women, Leymah Gbowee and Tawakkul Karman, from Yemen.

EXERCISE ON YOUR WILLINGNESS TO SACRIFICE

Write down three activities you are willing to sacrifice in order to pursue more fully the goal(s) to which you've committed yourself.

1._____

2._____

3._____

If you've done all the exercises in this book, consider yourself on the threshold of truly great accomplishments, provided you continue to act on the information. You've defined what you truly desire in life. Good going.

Look back over the exercises you've completed throughout the book as often as possible and consider whether any part needs revision as you continue to strive and move in your desired direction. Make sure you are on track. Never give up -- the road ahead may be full of thorns, but who better to embark on this journey of personal exploration and achievement than one as eager and prepared as you are to succeed!

Take action and prepare for greatness!

Those you will encounter in the following pages have all achieved great personal or professional success. Some of them may have started out with some of the challenges that you now face. Their examples are important because they did not settle for mediocrity; each of them knows what it takes to set and achieve goals. They could have accepted broken lives and broken dreams as their lot in life, but they did not. They knew that there was something better and that they had the capacity to reach out and touch it. You will find nuggets of wisdom aplenty from these ordinary people whose dedication and commitment to their goals have made them extraordinary in their achievements. From generous hearts, they share their secrets with you as you embark on your own journey into the zone of achievement, success, and peace of mind.

12
MORE TIPS FROM SUCCESSFUL PEOPLE

BETTY M. WILSON, Vice President, Director of Taxes and Assistant Secretary, ITT FINANCIAL CORPORATION, St. Louis, Missouri, U.S.A..

The qualities, character traits, and habits that have been instrumental in helping me achieve my goals are: Honesty, integrity, reliability, constancy, perseverance, and a genuine concern for other human beings. Developing relationships based on trust. Giving due credit to others, empowering and rewarding those who work with you.

I am a firm believer that people rise to the expectations of their leaders. I expect a great deal from those who work with me, but I provide them with opportunities to achieve and be recognized for their achievements. I define and communicate my expectations, and then I delegate and empower my staff, always aware that follow-up and feedback are the keys to their success. My goals have always included the creation of an atmosphere where each individual can perform up to his or her highest level of ability, and be rewarded for performance. No one is an island, and no one is successful in a vacuum. My success is dependent upon the success of those who work with me, as much as it is upon my own personal knowledge and expertise.

Coming out of college in 1969, I entered the CPA profession with (a major accounting firm) in St. Louis. I spent 6 years there, the last two as a Tax Manager. I experienced sexual harassment, discrimination, and unfair treatment almost constantly. When I took my issues to the Partner in charge, he told me "you are the first woman we have had to deal with in management, and we just don't know how to handle it" -- that was an understatement to say the least! After six years of what felt like beating my head against a brick wall, I left the firm and took my current job at ITT Financial. There has been some discrimination here and a few instances of what today would be called harassment. In spite of the obstacles, I have experienced a great deal of success. In 1988 I received the Harold S. Geneen Award for Individual Achievement (ITT's highest achievement award).

I am troubled by the current trend in the corporate world to squeeze more and more work out of fewer people. Corporate powers seem to be ignoring the human aspects of organizations, and treating people as if they were just commodities to be used and then thrown aside. I firmly believe that for long-term success, we must step back from today's trend of caring only about the bottom line and begin once again to care about the individuals who make up our organizations. After all, the organization is only as good as its product which depends on the "people" making that product and distributing it to the ultimate customer.

What does success mean? Many people define success on the basis of titles and material things. The "he who has the most toys wins" mentality is rampant in business. I personally believe that peace of mind is more important than money. Success for me is knowing that I am doing the very best job that I am capable of doing, that I treat those who work with me with respect and fairness at all times, and that I have not been dishonest with anyone, including myself. At times it seems that the "good guys" always lose when it comes to money and material success, but I continue to believe that good will prevail in the end. I am not personally willing to give in to the pressures of success at the expense of my integrity. To be revered for my integrity and rewarded for my efforts, my achievements, and my management skills is the ultimate "success" for me!

> **He who would accomplish little must sacrifice little;
> he who would achieve much must sacrifice much;
> he who would attain highly must sacrifice greatly.**
>
> - James Allen

MARCEL BARBEAU, painter/sculptor - Montreal, Quebec, Canada.

For me success means, first, personal and artistic achievement; that is to say the joy of doing what I am best suited to do - visual arts, and to accomplish works I am fully satisfied with, works in which I am true to myself and in which I feel I am able to surpass myself, to do the best paintings or the best sculptures that I can do at the moment that I do them. Second for me, comes the social achievement of these works, that is to say, recognition of the artistic quality of my works by my friends and peers, by experts and by the public. But I know that I always remain the first viewer or spectator of my work and that I must be fully satisfied with my work before I can enjoy the appreciation of others. It means that it wouldn't be an achievement for me to obtain social recognition and success in my career with works of art with which I am not fully satisfied myself.

The qualities which may have helped me in achieving success in my work and career are faith in my vocation, my work, my sense of what is ideal, my willpower, my persistence, even my stubbornness to pursue this vocation and this ideal in spite of economic and social obstacles such as ignorance, loneliness and doubts about myself. But I believe that my first quality was to be able to recognize that my personal strength was in what often appears as a weakness in our society, my sensitivity and my capacity to express this sensitivity visually through painting and sculpture and to understand that one can build even on weaknesses and negative events in one's life.

In this, my master, Paul Emile-Borduas, was very helpful as he gave me confidence in myself, recognizing some talent in my early works and advising me to become an artist. Other qualities and character traits which have helped me include my permanent dissatisfaction with myself, my work and my environment and my career which lead me to constantly research new challenges and enlarge my horizons. First, this has made me more and more uncompromising towards my works and their artistic and technical qualities. Thus, I always reject "easy-ness" and repetition which lead to stagnation both in one's work and career. This continual dissatisfaction also led me to always question myself and my work and to get out of my discipline and out of my home town, Montreal, to explore the rest of Canada and to go abroad to discover new works of art, new artistic and social milieus, other artistic and intellectual disciplines, like philosophy, poetry, the physical sciences, dance and music, to meet with other intellectuals and artists and exchange with them experiences and encounters which always proved to be most stimulating both intellectually and artistically. In addition these encounters often were helpful in the development of my career.

Another personality trait which may have been helpful to me, is that, being very proud and coming from a lower social class, and having become an orphan when I was very young, I developed the willpower to take my destiny in my own hands. Early in life, I became conscious of the need to be responsible for myself and to never count only on others, on dealers, for example, for the development of my career, but to do things for myself and for my career.

In fact, I started working after school and during weekends when I was 10 years old. Even at that age, I was quite realistic about how to conduct my career and developed a good capacity for work. Early in my career, I developed the habit of working regularly at my art, often 7 days a week. I feel that this kind of hard work is essential for one to become and remain a professional artist and to create a significant work of art.

Being both from a lower class, from a minority group in Canada and from a country which doesn't have the economic power and cultural influence of dominant countries such as the United States or France, made it more difficult to obtain international recognition. From a financial point of view, my original social class made it more difficult to work full time as an artist and to travel and work in major artistic centers as much as necessary for the development of an artist's work and career. From a social point of view, the fact that I did not study in a classical college, limited my peer group and made it more difficult to establish relationships with those in power in artistic institutions and universities and to develop a market among those of the upper class to which the more influential art collectors belong.

In the fifties, I felt that being from a minority ethnic group was also a handicap; it soon appeared to me that, in Canada, it was a less important handicap than being from a lower social class. In fact, the first institution to which I was invited to teach or speak was an English speaking university, Bishop University, and the first museum to organize an important show of my work was the Winnipeg Art Gallery and my works are in museums all over Canada.

Being from a small country which has nearly no influence on the art scene and on the art market made it more difficult to get the attention of people in power and to attract the attention of powerful art collectors abroad. This situation was an incentive to be more rigorous towards myself, my work and the conduct of my career. At 67 years, I still pursue my career and keep on exhibiting in Canada and abroad. Even though my work keeps receiving more and more attention both in Canada and abroad I am keenly aware of the fact that I still have a lot to learn and that pursuing an artistic career is an ongoing process that is never totally realized.

When I was still a student, my master, Borduas strongly advised me to adopt a professional attitude towards art and to always use the best materials and tools even if they were expensive. He also taught me to be very demanding toward myself, to always be true to myself, and to keep on working with the highest conscientiousness towards my own work and to never look for public approval. He further told me that social success would eventually come. I followed this advice which proved to be wise indeed. Later on, my friend the French philosopher of art and art critic Charles Delloye, supported this advice by encouraging my attitude toward research. Many years later, Dr. Stern from Dominion Gallery and my wife Ninon also gave good advice in recommending that I remain realistic towards the art market and that I do not increase the prices of my work too fast. Since I followed this advice, I never had to face a dramatic decline in the demand for my works. The good advice and the moral support of these people and of some other friends have also been very important to me.

I plan to continue pursuing my artistic research as much as possible while developing new projects for exhibitions in Canada and abroad, particularly in France and Europe where I recently received new recognition. I feel that it is the best way to keep my mind young and alive. One of my major desires is to create a major monumental sculpture in a major public place -- which of course does not only depend on myself!

LILLIAN VERNON, founder of The Lillian Vernon Corporation, New Rochelle, New York, U.S.A.

1. *Make time for yourself and your family.*
2. *Surround yourself with the best people possible.*
3. *Be open to new ideas and better ways to do things.*
4. *Be prepared to take risks.*
5. *Like what you do and like what you sell.*
6. *Don't dwell on your mistakes or setbacks - but instead learn and grow from them and then move on. Never let your mistakes defeat or discourage you.*
7. *Don't try to do it all - delegate!*
8. *Don't grow too fast without the proper systems and people in place to handle it.*
9. *Don't be afraid of computer technology that can help make your business more efficient.*
10. *Don't spend more money than you have - set realistic budgets and stick to them. Keep your debts manageable.*

DAVID SUZUKI, geneticist, broadcaster, lecturer, author, and president of The David Suzuki Foundation, Vancouver, B.C., Canada.

Useful qualities - I think my willingness to work hard, long hours is the most important.

Character traits - In my work, I think genuine curiosity and interest in new ideas is critical.

Habits - Must be willing to meet hard deadlines.

I think another important aspect is love and family. Without my wife, children and parents (both sets), I would be much diminished.

I should emphasize that "success" to me is not measured in economic terms but in terms of having a purpose in life and striving to achieve it.

IONA V. CAMPAGNOLA, broadcaster, former federal cabinet minister and past president of the Liberal Party; Courtenay, B.C., Canada.

I suspended geography (I was a northern British Columbian) and negative stereotyping of my gender from my earliest consideration as impediments to achievement. I sought an eclectic education, continuing to find means to learn to the present day. I do not consider personal comfort or affluence to be worthy goals for a well-lived life, earning only what is sufficient to my basic needs, enabling me to focus my activities and energies, toward domestic politics, global peace, world development, human rights and women's equality. My perception of success is to see gradual improvement in the common good of the Human Family.

JOHNNY ESAW is Vice President, Broadcast Services, of the Edelman Houston Group (Toronto, Canada). He has over three and half decades experience as a broadcaster and sports commentator and is recognized as a driving force behind the great financial success of amateur figure skating in Canada.

The basis for my success included many of the following practices: Never refuse the first job you are offered. You will learn so much more while working, observing and listening than you will while searching for something more ideal.

Save something, however little, from every paycheck. It's surprising how these small sums, even those that are minute, seem to mount and help you achieve financial independence.

As a young person you must try to shape your destiny by thinking of what you want to be (in general terms) thus eliminating time that might be spent on areas that amount to little more than a waste of time.

In each position, through various means, i.e., professionally and socially, try to meet and know your superiors. They will then be more aware of what you are doing; so pay increases come easier and thus advancement.

Never work by the clock and don't be too shy about being seen on the job after hours and on weekends. The word spreads around about this positive work ethic.

The foregoing creates greater increases for which your case is partially made for while seeking any increases, your record and reasonable attitude puts the onus on your superiors.

Learn what the responsibilities are at every level so you can widen your dimensions because stepping in at the right place and time could be a major turning point in your career.

Humility and honesty are the two most valuable characteristics one can exhibit and in fact, can become your own personal trademark.

Your eyes and ears should be focused on the level above you because this is your target. It makes it much easier for your superiors to make a decision on filling a position at the next level.

When you do achieve a position at the management level, you should deal with each of your employees on a one-to-one basis. You outline each other's responsibilities. You must keep an eye on each employee and each one will become a hard-working, loyal member of your staff. Thus, you will be the winner.

As an employer, from time-to-time you should do each employee a favour i.e., give them a half-day off because they have been working so hard.

In salary negotiations, you should add an extra few dollars - a perk of any sort - tell them to take someone out for dinner and bring you the receipt personally. It is amazing how often an employee will go that extra mile for a perk.

If an employee decides to leave, you must never implore them to stay. In fact, you advise them to think about the new offer very carefully because once they have left, your policy prohibits them from returning.

In management, you must do everything to find out what the opposition are doing. What are their short and long range plans? When you negotiate, you take advantage of your opponent's weaknesses and dwell on them - conversely you dwell on the advantages of doing business with you i.e., your past experience, future plans and your track record.

If possible, form a partnership both sharing in the gains but with you guaranteeing the losses.

If the product is of a high profile and costly, involve your president or chairman in part of the discussion. This always has some impact on the seller.

You might offer to purchase on the long-term or build in some escalating options. These conditions make it difficult for the seller or your competition to make a direct comparison.

You must always be on the lookout for new, young, fresh talent. This will give your department new energy. It will keep the veterans looking over their shoulders and hustling when they might otherwise let you down and become less productive.

Your staff meetings must tell it like it is. If the company is not pleased, or if it is having a good year, you must say so.

You advise your employees that you are working on their behalf to improve their benefits, meal allowances, per diem, car mileage, etc..

Success is based on several objectives you have reached.
- Build a successful department - dependability, loyalty, quality products that deliver a profit margin.
- Live within a realistic budget.
- Produce products and properties that are publicly recognized and produce positive media support.
- Create a level of business friendship with property owners who in turn become obliged to continue your association despite the overtures from "across the street".
- Your success can often be measured by the requests for your services as a speaker to business and social groups. This is one of the most realistic yardsticks.
- Because of the demands on your time for volunteer work i.e., United Way, Hospital campaigns etc., you must always make it known that you are giving of your time with the blessing of your company.
- Never let the objectives of the company be achieved at a cost to your family!

BARBARA COULTISH, founder/president of Barbara Coultish Talent and Model Management, Victoria, B.C., Canada.

Advice I would give to aspiring entrepreneurs: Be determined, have a strong business plan. Investigate your market thoroughly and keep a positive attitude!

I look at the strong months as benefits from our effort and the weaker months as pulling your team together to create new ideas and incentives.

Believe in your success! Learn from your contacts and listen to your clients. Be open to new ideas and input from employees and remember to pat them on the back. You'll be amazed how much more a person will give if you take the time to acknowledge their effort. Make them a strong team. It's harder for the competition to beat a company's successful team than to beat one successful business person. I love to learn and learn some more. I feel you can't take in too much business or personal growth information. Everything will help towards *your goal. I also feel you must treat people with respect; and I don't think there is a need for gossip or bad attitudes. (Unfortunately this is a known factor in our industry). I feel competition makes a strong team stronger!*

Success to me means a feeling of complete satisfaction and happiness with your family and loved ones, your friends, health, lifestyle and chosen career. It's certainly a tough challenge but well worth the effort it takes to make sure that all areas of your life are treated equally.

My future plans are to continue building my library, attending quality seminars and joining one or two more business organizations as well as volunteering! I'm a member of 5 organizations now and they take up about 10 hours of my time per month helping out or sitting on their boards. Those ten hours of service per month have helped further my career better than 100 hours in the office ever could. I have met hundreds of people and word of mouth is the best promotional tool there is!

JOHN BAGLOW, M.A., Ph.D. Writer, Trade Unionist - Ottawa, Ontario, Canada.

Success is not a matter of character, habits, qualities, etc., leading to the fulfillment of individual goals, self-advancement, etc., at least not to me. Real success in my opinion means changing society, which is a collective enterprise. Every committed, engaged person is successful in that sense....If we look at individual success, I believe that this society values some kinds of success over others. A person who suffers prolonged torture in a Guatemalan jail and through good fortune and determination makes it to Canada as a refugee is wildly successful in a way that I will never be. Ditto a woman who withstands sexual assault and over time is once again able to live a creative, positive and caring life free from fear and nightmare.

RITA MAE BROWN, author; Afton, Virginia, U.S.A.. Her books include: The Hand that Cradles the Rock, 1971; Rubyfruit Jungle, 1973; and Starting From Scratch: A Different Kind of Writer's Manual, 1988. TV Series include: I Love Liberty, 1982 and Long Hot Summer.

To be successful watch the donut not the hole!

JOHN CRISPO, Ph.D. Professor of Political Economy, Faculty of Management, University of Toronto, Ontario, Canada.

The key to whatever success I have had is fairly simple and straightforward. For as long as I can remember I have been true to myself and my convictions.

As a university professor, I early acquired tenure which enabled me to speak out without fear or favour, a luxury few people enjoy.

While I am sure I would have done better financially by selling my mind (and soul) to one interest group or another I have chosen to remain detached and therefore free.

On balance it has been very worthwhile.

MICHAEL WALKER, economist, journalist, broadcaster, consultant, university lecturer and public speaker. Executive Director of The Fraser Institute, Vancouver, B.C., Canada.

I hope your readers won't think me megalomaniacal when I say that my goal in life is to change the world and in as much as that is the case, and since I have not yet been successful, I have to measure my achievements rather relative to the achievement of certain objectives which contribute to achieving what my goal is. At the Fraser Institute we every year go through a strategic planning exercise in which we review our mission, set the objectives which are, during that year, related to the achievement of our mission, assess the obstacles that we will encounter in achieving those objectives and then devise action plans designed to deal with the obstacles which prevent us from achieving our goal during that period. It is very difficult for me to separate my own personal objectives and action plans from those of the Institute since the Institute is my life's work.

From the point of view of personal traits and characteristics, I was very fortunate to grow up in a household where hard work and determination were applauded and where there was a high expectation of achievement and I would have to say that to the extent that I have made any modest gains in achieving my goals it has been by relentlessly pursuing every opportunity that has been available to follow the action plans which are associated with our objectives. If there is one aspect of this relentless pursuit that I would think is important it is the fact that I am personally committed to the mission of the Institute and to changing society to be more market orientated and less determined by coercive institutions like, for example, large government.

On a personal level I note that you are exploring...the problem of minority groups getting ahead in the world. I would just note that this strikes a sympathetic chord in my own case because having grown up in Newfoundland and being a proud Newfoundlander I often encounter stereotypical reactions. Almost invariably when I'm being introduced to a group, for example, the Chairman feels that some reference to a Newfie joke is appropriate without, in most cases, realizing that this amounts almost to a kind of racist characterization. Suffice to say that the stereotype most people have of Newfoundlanders is not compatible with the image of the Executive Director of a think tank and one is subtly aware of this on an ongoing basis. However, I would say that the marvelous thing about our society in North America is that whether people have these stereotypes in the back of their minds or not, our system provides us all with the opportunity to overcome the stereotypes by personal conduct. I think the clear message for those who are part of groups who are often characterized by stereotypes is to achieve what you can and be judged by your achievements in spite of the stereotypes. I think that the last thing we should demand is separate treatment because, apart from the fact that it denigrates those who have achieved without 'affirmative action', it confirms the stereotype that the group couldn't achieve without the help.

In terms of personal habits and so on, I think that the most important ingredient of whatever small achievement I've had is hard work. At the moment I typically start my day at 6:30 a.m. I work at home for several hours in solitude before going to my office where I will work typically until 6:00 or 6:30 in the evening. On most days, after having eaten supper, I work for another hour or so before playing a game of squash and rounding out the evening by watching the late news broadcast and reading a few pages of a book before retiring usually around midnight or shortly thereafter.

GERALD GREENWALD, Chairman and Chief Executive Officer, United Airlines, Chicago, Illinois, U.S.A. United Airlines is the largest company in the United States with a majority of its stock owned by its employees. UAL generated $14.5 billion in revenues in 1993; its United Airlines subsidiary employs more than 76,000 men and women. Jerry Greenwald graduated *cum laude* from Princeton University's Woodrow Wilson School and received a master's in economics from Wayne State University. He previously served in leadership positions at Ford Motor Company (from 1957 to 1979), at Dillon Read & Company (1991-1993) and as president of Olympia & York Developments (1993-1994).[5]

I'm a believer in employee empowerment, but I want to see it linked to action. My view is that you can tell people all you want that they've got a stake in the company but they'd rather have a share of stock.

That's the way United looked at reform. From our perspective, merging looked more like a way to acquire someone else's headaches, and downsizing was no better.

So we sold the company -- to ourselves.

Our aim is to capture the spirit of "Mom and Pop, Incorporated," the corner grocery store model of customer service, when every time you went into a store you met across the counter an owner. Now, multiply that ethic of ownership across a complete company. Go beyond the rhetoric that in a service industry like ours, our employees are our strongest asset, and put that principle to the test.

Look up in your Webster's the word "employee." You'll see that the word has a Latin root that meant a person "involved" or "engaged" in an enterprise. That way of looking at employees hasn't always been popular.

Legend has it that Henry Ford used to complain, "Why is it when I only want a pair of hands, I get a whole human being?" Well, maybe that's the way it seemed at the beginning of the mass production era, but not today. We're learning that after all the head is handy.

We want our people to be engaged, energized, and alert to ways to serve the customer and do their work better. And in that effort, we happen to think that

---

[5]* Remarks (edited) by Gerald Greenwald, Chairman and CEO of United Airlines, given to the Economic Club of Chicago (October 18, 1994).

intelligence is an asset, not an impediment.

"Our people are our capital." Is that really such a new idea? Maybe it was when W.A. Patterson, CEO of United Airlines, said it back in 1934. Back then in the airline industry, it was an easier business to be in -- more regulation, less competition. But as different as things are today, what Patterson said still holds true. What would he think about the new United -- and the way we're working to re-write the rules on labor and management?

United by no means has the sole patent on the kind of empowerment I'm talking about. Consider Avis -- and the special operation they're running now with 600 people -- and not a single supervisor. Avis has given its employees the power to make angry customers happy -- authority to write checks, to approve free rental cars -- to do whatever it takes to correct the problem.

It's the same equation: Happy passengers equals profits.

Now, most companies would be terrified to give their people that kind of autonomy. They'd worry that after the first 24-hours, there'd be nothing left in the cash drawer. But what Avis has discovered is that giving its owners the "power of the purse" has produced restraint and results.

It's a question I've asked myself about our own company:

Are we a company that makes room for entrepreneurs? Do we chew them up and spit them out? Or do we take advantage of each individual's gut sense of what works?

Bob Galvin's company knows what I mean. At Motorola, last year, they had a woman in their Philippine plant, a worker on the semi-conductor assembly line, who saved the company a quarter-of-a-million dollars. She knew a better way to make the product, and management gave her the power to try it out.

Service companies have the same need.

I want to share a story with you, without naming names. We have a customer service agent on a critical run, one with a lot of regular, high-profile passengers. This agent is an eccentric. Whatever else you can say about him, he makes an impression. Over the years, he has built a rapport with our regular passengers. Whatever they needed, he got it done -- and they came to swear by him. With his co-workers, things were a bit different. They preferred to swear at him.

Now, this fellow was not easy to work with, and he'd be the first to tell you. He had a fistful of bad performance reviews to prove it. Not too long after I got to United, he got his final "last chance," and was given notice that he was being let go.

About that time, my phone started to ring. Celebrities, the wives of CEOs, people in high places -- all defending this guy. I didn't know this fellow, but we decided right then: Whoever he is, he's not going anywhere.

I learned a couple of lessons from that episode. First, what the company means to the public -- can come down to a single employee.

Second, it made me ask, "What is our priority as a company: To make things easy on ourselves, on our organization -- or to serve the customer?"

The customer service agent in question is back on the job -- but make no mistake: We're going to work a little harder with him, taking off the rough edges. I'm not saying that United owns the patent on how to change corporate culture. What works for us may not be right for everyone else. My point is simply this:

When we have exhausted all the external avenues of change -- when we've run the gamut with the current wave of corporate make-overs -- can we say that we've made the most of the people who make our companies work?

In the same way it took Nixon to open China, it may be time for business to raise tough issues about the future of industrial America. It may be the right moment for management, for the best of reasons -- for bottom line reasons -- to look at empowering our employees. Some companies, like United, should look at employee ownership as a tool to boost performance, productivity and profit.

NORMAN REBIN, entrepreneur, corporate trainer and industry consultant; Altona, Ontario, Canada.

Success to me means balance - creating harmony between the physical, mental, emotional and spiritual dimensions of one's being. This means building relationships, personally, and building relevance, professionally, and always keeping the balance.

The most important feature or value supporting any goal or success I've had, is that I try to remember that I hold my life, in trust, for those who preceded me and those who will follow. That's my life's moral and my epitaph. It reminds me that the inner voice (conscience) is more important than the braying of a thousand critics, and gives me focus. I also try to keep conscious of the 'treasure of time' - each moment counts, so I don't waste it.

The other feature of my 'success' is my unbridled curiosity - about my creator, about my colleagues, and about my world. To 'learn' is not to 'yearn', so

I never stop searching for knowledge.

You mention success of minority members, such as the distinguished David Suzuki. Well, I am a Doukhobor minority member, and I will die one. Doukhobors, as you know, constitute one of the smallest, but, most pervasive movements in the world. Our drive for world harmony, ecological harmony, gendoral harmony, geographical harmony, and cultural harmony is truly the ideal whose time has come (the next millennium). Too many minority members feel that they have to 'transcend' the burden of their heritage. To me, that's philosophical pap and mental manure.

My minority status gave me an 'edge' on life! It fostered in me the belief that God's greatest gift to a human is to give him/her a sense of their own unique, individual, being. Doukhoborism taught me that when you're a minority member you don't have to carry the garbage of majority masses on your shoulders, but, that you can find a uniquely better way. What burden is that? Once, only, when I was a young man smitten by a bright, beautiful, buxom, Anglo-Saxon wasp majority member (my now wife of 34 years, Delva) I strove to dramatize the fact that perhaps I was a misunderstood, sometimes maligned, minority Doukhobor. Delva interrupted my flow of 'self-imposed' martyrdom to ask, "So what? I love you. I don't know your group. If I marry you, it will be you I marry, not your group! Get it?" I got it! I never forgot. Whether Japanese or Jew, Doukhobor or Rastafarian - you are the messenger and the message. Let's stop martyring our groups because of our personal failures. And let's compliment ourselves, not our groups, for our personal successes. No scapegoats and no self-effacement!

LANCE J. STRAUSS, President of Lance J. Strauss Enterprises, Inc., Carmel, California, U.S.A.

1. Never give up!
2. Treat employees and customers fairly, as you would want to be treated.
3. Ensure that your employees are compensated fairly and give them unexpected cash bonuses from time to time.
4. Praise your employees as much as possible.
5. Be honest at all times.
6. Operate your business defensively. Think about all the things that could hurt your business and develop strategies to combat potential problems before they occur.

7. Read as much as you can get your hands on (I read a minimum of 4 to 5 newspapers a day and several magazines a week).
8. Keep an eye on your competition at all times.
9. Never stay stagnant. Constantly look for that next new business idea. Remember, nothing is forever. Times change, people change, consumer buying habits change.

To advance myself, in addition to my voracious reading, I continually attend conferences and seminars in my field.

With respect to my personal background, I am married with 2 children. I am a graduate of the U.S. Naval Academy and hold a Master's degree in Management. Before starting my business career, I was a Navy Pilot. My information business activities have been written about in over 40 magazines and newspapers and I have appeared as a guest on over 100 radio and TV talk shows. With over 35,000 customers, my 900 service bureau is the largest in North America. In fact, we have more customers than all of my 100 or so competitors combined!

LAWRENCE IWASAKI, award-winning hair stylist and proprietor of Maison Lawrence Hair Salon, Burnaby, B.C., Canada.

Qualities to achieve goal - to get as much knowledge as possible then to practice and attain goals by competitions.

Re: first Canadian champion 1956. Repackage yourself so that manufacturers can use you as image maker for their product - don't lose your uniqueness but you do have to fit white man's business world! I have been on stage and road for 30 years for the largest and best manufacturers of beauty salon products in the world. I hope I have contributed to raising standards in our trade! I still work with young people, governments and our association. You must have faith in yourself but you have to earn a cash basis for yourself to become credible to the business world! I was the first to receive $250,000 fund from the (Canadian) federal government small business loan program on my reputation and credibility in our business community.

WILLIAM E. SIMON, former Secretary of the Treasury of the United States of America. After holding the position of Secretary of the Treasury for three years, Mr. Simon left government and launched a series of successful business enterprises. In 1979, along with his partner Ray Chambers, he launched Wesray Corporation which was a pioneer in mergers and acquisitions. Mr. Simon is currently Chairman of William E. Simon & Sons, a private merchant bank with offices in New Jersey, Los Angeles and Hong Kong, which he formed with his two sons in 1988.

Clearly, [success] always requires hard work, determination and some plain old good luck. If I have any "secret," it is having firm principles, and being a compass rather than a weather vane along life's highway.

YASSEMI MEHRANGUIZ, painter, Tehran, Iran. Awards: 1979 Golden Medal "Accademia Italia"; 1983 Golden Medal: Int'l Parliament, U.S.A., 1988 Accademia d'Europa-Premio: Palma d'oro d'Europa; 1990 Golden Medal "European Banner of the Arts."

I have to note that my father, Ali Akbar Yassemi, was one of the greatest artists of our country and it has been a great honor for me to have him as my father and teacher. He loved painting and it was an end for him, not the means. He had a sensitive look and even the most seemingly trivial events of life could turn into an attractive scene under his powerful brush strokes. And this, I think, is what can differentiate an artistic look from an ordinary one, i.e., to see life from a different angle and to notice things which are normally overlooked.

His works and way of life have been a great inspiration for me and have helped me to acquire a keen sense for art since my childhood. I learned the fundamentals of painting with my father and later entered the College of Fine Arts at the University of Tehran, after his untimely death. After completing college, I started working in all the three fields of oil painting, water colors, and especially pencil work. I have participated in many exhibitions in Europe and the U.S.A. and I've also received some prizes.

However, receiving prizes and recognition has never been my goal in painting. My first prize came to me quite unexpectedly. Apparently the Museum of Modern Art of Iran had sent one of my works to Italy, and I received a prize for it, not knowing myself that I had participated in any competition! Later one of the universities in Italy helped me to exhibit my works in international events under their auspices. I was fortunate to have such a contact at a time when Iran was engaged in the terrible war with Iraq. Painting was never my job. I worked as a cartographer in the Institute of Geography at the University of Tehran for 20 years and now I have retired and can devote more time to my love, painting. I paint for my own enjoyment and I don't necessarily devote myself to conveying any particular message through my works or to comply with people's tastes. However, I take the technical aspects of the work very seriously and I am not much interested in the new-wave, fashionable modern art or abstract paintings.

Real success, in any kind of work, comes only with a genuine and honest feeling of love and devotion that cannot be forged by technical advancement, fame or material gain. In addition, patience, hard work, precision and correct drawing techniques are the basic tools for every artist's success!

JORGE SALAZAR-CARRILLO, economist, director of the Department of Economics, Florida International University, U.S.A.

The formula of success that has worked for me is a deep religious commitment to the betterment of this world, and the persistence to keep driving forward whenever I perceive an opportunity for change. This defined a road full of hard work, but since my purpose is transcendental, I have thoroughly enjoyed every moment of it, and nothing has disappointed me.

ED MCMAHON, broadcaster, television personality and president of Ed McMahon Productions, California, U.S.A.

My approach to success was helped greatly by some advice my father gave me. He said, "to set attainable goals and achieve them." He went on to point out that what that gave you was great satisfaction, and then he said, "you'll be able to go after and achieve your next goal."

I grew up in a household where hard work seemed to be the order of the day. I picked up a "work ethic" that has stayed with me throughout my life. I also learned something great in the Marine Corps...and that was to always be on time and to be ready to do what you had to do when you got there. Being a broadcaster has helped me understand the importance of time.

I don't think there is anything more important in life than to wake up in *the morning and know that you're going to do the best you can that day, both professionally and personally.*

DENTON A. COOLEY, M.D., Surgeon-in-chief, Texas Heart Institute, Houston, Texas, U.S.A.

A career can be chosen by chance or by direction; my own choice probably resulted from both. Success, however, leaves nothing to chance. Only through education, perseverance, and hard work can goals be reached and success attained.

Education plays an essential role in achieving success. In my opinion, high school graduation should not mark the end, but the beginning of a person's schooling. Whether in the trades or in academics, an advanced education brings one's dreams infinitely closer to fruition. Without such a commitment, however, these same dreams may never become a reality.

People often ask me how I achieved such success; why was I so lucky? The answer is simple: the harder I worked, the luckier I became. I have never encountered anyone whose success was due only to fortune or mere desire. Invariably, high achievers work harder and are more determined than their peers. Everyone possesses the potential for some measure of greatness; the choice whether or not to fulfill this potential belongs to the individual.

The formula for success is simple: exercise your imagination, set goals, and persevere. Let nothing distract you from your purpose, and ultimately, you will reap the benefits of your actions.

PIERRE DIOUF, Senegalese Ambassador to Canada, Ottawa, Canada.

I believe that to a great extent any personal success depends on the clarity of the objective one sets, on the strategies and tactics used to achieve that objective, and on the necessary means and the desire to succeed. In short, one needs to be organized and methodical.

Luck, some might say fate or fortune, and the human and natural environment may play a decisive part, as one cannot do anything alone.[6]

---

6 Translated from French into English by Hubert Migeon of Vice Versa Translation, Victoria, British Columbia, Canada.

SIR RICHARD BRANSON, Entrepreneur, Virgin Group

Richard Branson started in the business world as a mail-order entrepreneur. A high school dropout, he has built hundreds of businesses, in fields as varied as hospitality, finance, airline, and space travel. Branson contributes frequently to newspapers and magazines, sharing the lessons he has learned over the years with those who yearn to turn their dreams into reality. He never allowed what others might see as deficits, such as his dyslexia, to rob him of the opportunity to attain his dreams. Yet, it is important to note that while he seems today the epitome of confidence and success the early years of his career were far from smooth sailing.

Branson Takes Risks

If your goal is to play it safe all the time, success is likely to elude you. Achieving goals often requires you to act even when you do not have a complete picture of what you might go through to achieve your goals. But if you do not start, then you are unlikely to confront the necessary challenges that will lead you to your goals. Sometimes, attaining success is a matter of eliminating obstacles and that means being comfortable with taking risks. Sometimes, taking a risk means that you are going to fall down on your face either because of your own lack of effective planning or because of unforeseen events. As Branson recounts,

> *One example of a decision that I would like to claim full benefit for would be our acquisition of the first Boeing 747, which came just before a rapid upturn in the secondhand market for 747s. On the other hand, I would like to blame the fact that 'Event" - the magazine we started up some years ago in competition with 'Time Out' - failed, not because we did not plan it or manage it carefully enough, but because something completely unexpected happened.*

Such failures will come but they are never a good reason to fold or give up because the lessons you learn from failure can help you do even better next time. Why throw away hard-earned lessons?

Be a Lover of Knowledge

Knowledge is the lifeblood of business. Think about it. The only reason you are paying thousands of dollars for a product may simply be because of your lack of knowledge -- of how to make it or where to get it -- meaning that the person with the knowledge and the necessary contacts, can translate that knowledge into a tidy profit. But having knowledge can benefit you in so many other ways, helping you to save money, work faster, achieve efficiencies and stay ahead of the competition. Taking risks does not mean just jumping into anything simply because it sounds good. As Branson advises,

> *The biggest risk any of us can take is to invest money in a business that we don't know. Very few of the businesses that Virgin has set up have been completely new fields. Admittedly, I started fresh - 'a virgin' - in the mail order record business, on the back of the abolition of retail price maintenance. Since then, however, the development of the Group has been through a linked series of investments, which I gather the business schools call vertical integration, but which I just call common sense. From the mail order business we went into retailing records, from the retailing of records we went into record production, through the setting up of the Virgin record label. We soon found that it was possible to negotiate music publishing rights as well as record rights with the same band, so we set up a music publishing company. Once we got past the very early stages, we realized that we were spending an awful lot of money on recording costs so we got into the recording studio business. When music videos became a necessary part of the marketing of records, we did not just make them and waste them, but began to distribute them ourselves. This got us into the video distribution business and it was a natural move to begin to acquire other products for video distribution.*

Getting to know your business is not necessarily always a matter of spending money. It may mean spending time at the library or at the computer, reading or listening to reports that many others might be taking for granted.

Be Prepared to Walk Away

Being persistent is good but being persistent does not mean that you have to flog a dead horse in the hope that it will suddenly come alive. Shooting for your dreams also means knowing when to pull back when something is not leading you in the direction you ought to be heading. If you commit yourself to a deal or a plan without the willingness to let go, you may find yourself stuck when in fact going in another direction might have been better for you and your project. It is with this in mind that Branson advises entrepreneurs to, "always be prepared to walk away." This is how Branson puts it:

> *It is wonderful how the knowledge that you are in a position to [walk away] can improve a deal. A recent example has been in our negotiation for the financing of a second 747. Had we been an airline like British Caledonian or British Airways, who 'have to be in the business' then the bankers would have asked for all sorts of security and they would have got it. However, because we were able to say to the bankers 'you are either going to lend us money without recourse to the rest of the Virgin Group or we are not going to bother buying a second aircraft' they have lent money just to the airline and enabled us to reduce the risk enormously.*[7]*

Start Small

There are many businesses that started out modestly but can now be counted among the giants in the business world. Some people think that having a fancy office or an expensive fleet of cars will enhance their image and lead to business success. True, image is important, but keep your eyes on the money. Reducing fixed costs can help you maneuver more freely when things are tough. In Branson's words,

> *First, keep overheads low....Second, as businesses grow, watch out for management losing touch with the basics - normally the customer....*

---

[7] The quotations above are excerpts from text by Richard Branson published in the Journal of General Management, Vol. 11, No. 2, Winter 1985 and was adapted from a talk given by Mr. Branson to the New Henley Management Course in October, 1985.

> *Thirdly, this 'keep it small' rule enables us to give more than the usual number of managers the challenge and excitement of running their own businesses.*

For those who want to take the entrepreneurial path, Branson is all encouragement. In his words, "Entrepreneurship is the beating heart. Entrepreneurship isn't about capital; it's about ideas. Entrepreneurship is also about excellence. Not excellence in awards or other people's approval, but the sort that one achieves for oneself by exploring what the world has to offer."[8]

KAREL HUSA, conductor; Ithaca, New York, U.S.A.. Mr. Husa was born in Prague in 1921. He went to Paris in the mid-'40s to study with Arthur Honegger, Nadia Boulanger, and Andre Cluytens and, in 1954, came to the United States to join the faculty of Cornell University. He has composed in all musical media (except opera) and his Music for Prague 1968 has made him one of the world's most frequently performed composers (with over 7,000 performances to date). He is the recipient of many awards and prizes, including the Pulitzer Prize, the Bilthoven (Holland) Contemporary Music Prize, a Kennedy Center-Friedham Award, the American Academy and Institute of Arts and Letters Award, and the Sudler International Award. His Concerto for Cello and Orchestra earned him the 1993 Grawemeyer Award.

> *In order to be successful at music composition, one has to have, in addition to talent, years of technical learning about how musical works are constructed - not only contemporary compositions but also those of the great composers of the past.*
>
> *To compete with other composers one has to try to be as good as they are or were. Only excellent works will survive, and we compete in concerts with giants such as Bach, Beethoven, Mozart and others, not only our contemporaries.*
>
> *We have to like our work and spend all our lives in it. We have to believe in ourselves and be strong to survive failures. We have to persevere every day, for there are difficult times in addition to good ones. Success keeps us going, failures are hard to accept but we have to put them behind us and keep going.*

---

[8] Richard Branson: Virgin Entrepreneur. *Success Magazine*. 2009.

Composers have to write an important number of works; some of them will be better than others and only the best survive. We have to accept the fact, that not every work will be a masterpiece. Some works will be successful immediately, others may have to wait.

Critical assessments or public acceptances are not always right (as we know from rejections of the masterpieces of the past) and we have to have the stamina to survive - sometimes for years - such judgments.

Success for me means personal satisfaction, that a work I have done has been accepted. It is also an encouragement to continue to work. Without strong technical preparation, a composer today cannot survive. Talent is not enough.

BARRY MORRIS GOLDWATER, former senator; Republican candidate for President of the United States, 1964. Received Presidential Medal of Freedom, 1986.

All the qualities, character traits, and anything good in my life, and career, can be summed up in a very few words. I was lucky enough to have a mother who taught me very early that the main attribute to keep me on track, was honesty.

I learned from her that honesty should be the prime quality of my life, and it always has been. No matter how old I get, she is always there, at my shoulder, reminding me, and God willing she will be there until I join her.

ELEANOR J. SMITH, chancellor of University of Wisconsin-Parkside. She holds a doctorate in African American history from the Union Institute in Cincinnati and bachelor's degrees in music education and education from Capital University in Columbus, Ohio. She also did graduate work at Ohio State University.

A commitment to my goals has always been a driving force for continuing to reach the target. A high level of integrity and a sense of honesty to myself and to others has been very much a part of my value system. Maintaining a positive outlook and a determination to make every experience a vehicle for growth and development has been critical in meeting the objectives set. I can't control what happens to me, but I can control how I respond. The space between what comes my way and my responses allows me to creatively control my life.

One's self-concept and perception is most important in dealing with the challenges that life brings. I have always tried to associate and surround myself with people with similar value systems, personal and professional agendas.

I am a lifelong learner, and I believe I am always becoming. I have the opportunity and obligation to continuously discover what is yet unexplored.

Although race and gender have had an impact on my life, I have not allowed the prejudices and lack of tolerance of others to determine my success or failure in reaching my goals. I believe I am the captain of this ship and I accept that responsibility with all my being.

The Honourable JEAN CHAREST, C.P., Former Member of Parliament for Sherbrooke, Quebec. Former leader of the Progressive Conservative Party (Canada). In June 1986, Mr. Charest was appointed Minister of State for Youth and became the youngest person to ever sit in the Cabinet. In the 1993 Conservative Party Leadership campaign, Mr. Charest came second to Prime Minister Kim Campbell who then appointed him Deputy Prime Minister of Canada, Minister of Industry & Science. Hon. Jean Charest also served as the 29th Premier of Quebec from 2003 to 2012.

One of the characteristics which I found to be essential to a career in political life is perseverance. Especially now [1995], the Progressive Conservative Party of Canada is faced with a challenge unparalleled in its long and prosperous history. Not only is it challenging to be the Member of Parliament for Sherbrooke, (Quebec) it is also a unique one to be the leader of a rebuilding political party.

Above all, I have found that honesty and authenticity are essential. For ten years now, the people of Sherbrooke have given me their trust and confidence in representing their concerns in the House of Commons. As a resident of Quebec's Eastern Townships myself, their concerns are also my concerns, and when I act on their behalf, I know the responsibility that goes along with being their elected Federal representative. I know that longevity in politics depends heavily upon being what you are and doing what you say; those who act like someone which they are not have short-lived stays in Ottawa.

I would also like to point out my strong views of a united Canada. Our shared Canadian identity can be categorized by one important word: freedom. In Canada, we have the freedom to work, study, and live in any part of the country. We have the freedom to learn two languages and the freedom to travel in any part of the world as a welcome and respected visitor because we are Canadian. In my mind, that is worth fighting for and it is keeping this in mind which also serves to inspire me in my everyday affairs.

I plan to continue travelling the country and talking to Canadians to see what they want from their politicians. It is my hope that through these discussions I will better be able to reflect their concerns within my party. My goal is none other than to lead a P.C. Party which is truly national and one which represents the needs and wishes of all Canadians regardless of what region of the country they live in.

DR. NORMAN E. BORLAUG, winner of the Nobel Peace Prize, 1970; Distinguished professor of International Agriculture, Texas A & M University, College Station, Texas, U.S.A.. Known as the father of the "Green Revolution" (which refers to the application of modern technology to agriculture in developing nations to increase food production dramatically), Dr. Borlaug served as an Associate Director of the Rockefeller Foundation for over 20 years, and as a consultant with the Food and Agriculture Organization (FAO) of the United Nations. He received honorary degrees from over 30 universities and was a member of the U.S. National Academy of Sciences, and honorary member of 10 foreign academies of science. Dr. Borlaug received dozens of academic, scientific, and achievement awards, including the Jefferson Award from the American Institute for Public Service, the U.S.A. Presidential Medal of Freedom, the Aztec Eagle from Mexico, and the Recognition Award of the Agricultural Institute of Canada.

Mine is a simple philosophy. To the young I say:
ON THE POSITIVE SIDE we have these "Do's"!
1. Educate and train yourself broadly.
2. Be optimistic and positive in outlook on life.
3. Give your best -- Motivation comes from within.
4. Be the best -- Become a leader for good.
5. Develop a concern for others.
6. Become a team player.
7. Nourish Common Sense.
8. Work hard.

9. Learn to play and relax.
10. Take good care of your body.
11. Remember it is difficult to construct.
12. Remember there have been many brilliant people in this world in previous generations -- Learn from history to avoid repeating the same mistakes.
13. Remember there is some force in this universe greater than humankind.

ALSO REMEMBER: If we prepare ourselves and work together we can build a better world for all.

ON THE NEGATIVE SIDE we have these "Don't's"!
1. Don't expect to build a better world without education.
2. Don't be a drop-out.
3. Don't be mediocre -- This way you cannot build a better world and mediocrity is in oversupply.
4. Don't become arrogant.
5. Don't forget the less fortunate.
6. Don't believe you alone can achieve much.
7. Don't become oversophisticated.
8. Don't underestimate the value and dignity of honest hard work.
9. Don't over play.
10. Don't become a slave...to drugs and/or alcohol.
11. Remember it's easy to destroy.

BUT REMEMBER ALSO: The world today is not all bad. There is more good than bad in it. More than 4 billion people live better than ever before. But we still have too many malnourished underprivileged -- Let's get to work and correct this....by work and sweat!

CAROL COLUMBUS-GREEN, women's control garment designer, former fashion model, president of Laracris Corporation (Intimate Apparel), Chicago, Illinois, U.S.A.

My idea (for shapewear) was generated through a personal need. When I could not find any attractive shapewear (girdles) on the market I realized that there was a niche and that I could design something better for women.
First I did a market research plan, then a business plan. I prototyped to find the best design. After a year of research and prototyping my first order came from Marshall Field's of Chicago. We are now in major department stores all around the country. I can only tell people who are aspiring to be entrepreneurs that there will be many problems and disappointments, but if they believe in their idea and work hard against adversity they can and will be successful.
My strongest support is a spiritual one. No matter how bleak things look my spirituality allows me to always believe in a positive outcome.

DR. NALIN J. UNAKAR, professor of Biological Sciences, Oakland University, Rochester, Michigan, U.S.A.

During my childhood my family and I suffered considerable hardship due to the displacement from Pakistan to India. We were refugees who were forced to leave Pakistan after the partition of India in 1947. This situation resulted in forcing my parents to start a new life at an advanced age with very little or no financial resources and a large family to support.
One of the major advantages that I and my siblings had was a strong commitment from our parents for education. My parents also believed in hard work and a disciplined life. These traits were very important for my success in life. There is no substitute for hard work, a disciplined approach and an appreciation for the ethical values in achieving carefully selected goals in life.
I strongly believe that my success, in the profession I selected, and the goals I set for myself, was mainly due to the hardship suffered in my childhood which made me more determined to achieve my goals.
In order to achieve my goals, I carefully charted my course of action and worked diligently toward fulfilling all my set expectations. As I said before, there is no substitute for hard work and commitment. I have been one of the fortunate individuals who has enjoyed good health, require very little sleep and have received total and unquestionable support from my family. I carefully

organize my schedule and try very hard to complete all the work on time as scheduled. I strongly believe that one should try to be one step ahead of others and complete tomorrow's work today and next week's work should be completed this week.

I also believe that one should take advantage of their own biorhythms. It is true that some individuals are very active and proficient during certain parts of a 24-hour day. One should take advantage of the time period which is most suitable for quality high productivity. I have followed the above stated habits and traits. In spite of my successful career, I still feel that there is much to be achieved in life and I continue to set new goals to be achieved.

As for what success means to me, I would like to state that not the success, but completing the task I set for myself is very fulfilling and satisfying. I am proud that in spite of the limited resources available during my prime age and a potentially bleak future, I have been able to achieve what I wanted to achieve and made some contributions to the world I live in.

GLADYS STYLES JOHNSTON, chancellor of University of Nebraska at Kearney, U.S.A. Chancellor Johnston's educational credentials include a bachelor's degree in Social Science from Cheyney University of Pennsylvania, a master's degree in educational administration from Temple University and a Ph.D. in educational administration and organizational theory and behaviour from Cornell University.

I believe that one's personal successes are grounded firmly on the relationships we have with others. Therefore, it is important to treat people kindly, fairly and with consideration. Power, and the exercise of that power, can be a good thing, but it must be used discreetly.

SIR GEORG SOLTI, music director laureate, Chicago Symphony Orchestra, Chicago, Illinois, U.S.A. Sir Georg Solti studied piano, composition and conducting with Béla Bartók, Erno Dohnányi, Kodaly and Leo Weiner. He served as conductor for the Budapest opera. In 1937, Toscanini selected him as his assistant at the Salzburg Festival. From 1979 to 1984, he served as Principal Conductor and Artistic Director of the London Philharmonic Orchestra and subsequently its Conductor Emeritus. Sir Georg Solti won 31 Grammy awards.

There is no substitute for sheer hard work, in achieving both personal and professional goals. The other important factors are both talent and a measure of good luck but it is dangerous to rely on either of these alone. There is no substitute for sheer industriousness.

CONSTANCE TOMKINSON (Lady Weeks), author, Chichester, West Sussex, England.

I am the daughter of Grace Tomkinson the novelist and was brought up in the shadow of her typewriter so I had no illusions about writing. I knew it was a very hard job. I got my experience writing plays that never got produced. I had some very near misses but I couldn't stand any more without winning so I changed with my mother's advice to writing in another form and hit the jackpot on the first go which surprised many critics who on the first book expected a complete beginner. But I had got my practice writing plays that never got produced. So my advice to all writers is to keep writing. That is the only way you will learn, so just keep writing and eventually you will get published.

DR. C.K. CHOU, former director, City of Hope National Medical Center, Duarte, California, U.S.A. B.S. (1968) Electrical Engineering, National Taiwan University; M.S. (1971) Electrical Engineering, Washington University; Ph.D. (1975) Electrical Engineering and Physiology, University of Washington; Postdoctoral Fellow (1975-1976) Department of Physiology and Biophysics. Dr. Chou has published over 130 papers and book chapters.

Work hard.

13

LEAVING YOUR FOOTPRINTS ON THE SANDS OF TIME

The single-minded pursuit of a goal, backed by proper preparation, invariably leads to success. But this same success that people crave has sometimes left a bitter pill in the mouths of those who attain it. Not a few people have reached the pinnacle of success only to ask: "Is that it?" "Why do I not feel fulfilled?"

Some drown their disappointment in drugs, sex, or other behaviors that put them on the downward path back to where they had struggled for years to depart.

Selfish or Selfless?

One means by which the great, the truly successful, are able to maintain an even keel, is not to focus only on themselves and seek to live solely for the pleasure that their success can access. Rather than worry endlessly about how big a house they should live in, what sports car they should drive each week, what exotic location they should choose for a vacation every six months, they realize that their success is a blessing and that the true joy of life is not just leading a life of selfishness but one of selflessness.

An Easy Way to Unload Your Stress

Novelist Charlotte Bronte knew whereof she spoke when she wrote: "Happiness quite unshared can scarcely be called happiness; it has no taste." And decades later, one of the most successful people, American talk how host and TV network owner Oprah

Winfrey, who has experienced the highs and lows of life, and talked to thousands of people from every station in life, has this advice for those who may be hurting inside despite all outward markers of success. She says, "If you're in pain, help someone else's pain and when you're in a mess, you get yourself out of the mess helping someone out of theirs."

Beyond the Fancy Car

All those whose ideas we cherish and follow, Confucius, Jesus Christ, Mohammed, Socrates, Plato, Gandhi, and Martin Luther King Jr., just to mention a few, are certainly not those who defined success simply by the size of one's bank account, the size of one's house, or the swiftness of one's car. These great ones challenge us to think deeply not only about ourselves, our needs and wants, but also about our relationships with others, our place in the community, and our potential contributions to making the world a better place, in short, what truly matters in life.

Your Legacy

So, having attained success, what would your legacy be? Would your legacy be one of seeking justice for the oppressed? Would your legacy include extending a helping hand in the quest for cures to the myriad diseases in the world? Would your legacy be the spreading of education and the elimination of ignorance from the planet?

Already, some have taken the lead. There are a number of highly successful people who have decided to contribute a substantial portion of their wealth towards making the world a better place. The Giving Pledge, initiated by Bill Gates and Warren Buffett, for example, encourages wealthy individuals to make a commitment to giving away most of their wealth to philanthropy. Those who have signed on to such initiatives may probably find that they sleep a little better than before.

Malcolm Gladwell, author of *Outliers*, generated a bit of controversy when he tried to compare two technological titans of the the early 21st century, Bill Gates and Steve Jobs. No one knows what arrangements the late Steve Jobs has made for his family to spend the billions of dollars he accumulated in life as a co-founder of the technology giant, Apple Incorporated. But Bill Gates' efforts, through the work of the Bill and Melinda Gates Foundation, include channeling funds towards solving intractable problems of disease around the world. On May 28, 2012, at a Toronto Public Library hosted dialogue, Gladwell stated:

> *I firmly believe that 50 years from now, [Bill Gates] will be remembered for his charitable work. No one will even remember what Microsoft is, and all the great entrepreneurs of this era. People will have forgotten Steve Jobs. There will be statues of Gates across the third world...there's a reasonable shot...because of his money, we will cure malaria.*

The world remembers the good and the bad alike. But those who are willing to extend a helping hand to those in need, those who are willing to give a hand up to a struggling person, those who do not consider only their own needs, are those that the world chooses to remember with a warm heart down through the generations.

The world awaits your contribution

American actress Rita Moreno, who, at the March on Washington for Jobs and Freedom on August 28, 1963, sat barely ten feet away when Dr. Martin Luther King Jr. addressed the crowd, speaks with insight when she says that, "being involved in something that is greater than you is what makes a person complete and whole."

There are many different ways by which successful people make an impact. It may even be that you will contribute your own new ideas to expand the avenues by which knowledge, wisdom, peace, and love, are spread around the world.

The planet has seen its share of atrocities. Here's hoping that your success will not add to the sum of the planet's woes but rather be a benefit to yourself and to those around you: your community, your country, your continent, and the wider world beyond.

Best wishes as you prepare for greatness!!!

BIBLIOGRAPHY

Bartlett, John. *Bartlett's Familiar Quotations*. Canada: Little Brown & Co., 1980.
Bennett, A. *How To Live On 24 Hours A Day*. New York: Cornerstone Library, 1962.
Bliss, Edwin C. *Getting Things Done*. New York: Bantam Books, 1976.
Browne, Harry. *How I Found Freedom in an Unfree World*. New York: Macmillan Publishing Co., 1973.
Carnegie, Dale. *Five Minute Biographies*. New York: Greenberg, 1937.
Carnegie, Dale. *How to Develop Self-Confidence and Influence People by Public Speaking*. New York: Pocket Books, 1956.
Carnegie, Dale. *How to Stop Worrying and Start Living*. New York: Simon and Schuster, 1948.
Carnegie, Dale. *How to Win Friends and Influence People*. New York: Pocket Books, 1982.
Chiu, Tony. L. A. "Law Gains a New Practitioner." Oct. 24, 1991. www.people.com
Clifford, Clark. *Counsel to the President: A memoir*. Peter Osnos, ed., Richard Holbrooke. Random House, 1991.
Collins, L. & Lapierre, D. *Freedom at Midnight*. New York: Avon Books, 1975.
Cosby, B. *Love and Marriage*. New York: Bantam Books, 1990.
Cousins, Norman. *Head First: the Biology of Hope*. New York: E.P. Dutton, 1989.
Cousins, Norman. *Human Options*. New York: Berkley Books, 1981.
Covey, S. *The 7 Habits of Highly Effective People: Powerful Lessons in Personal Change*. New York: Simon and Schuster, 1989.
Cuddy, Amy. *Your Body Language Shapes Who You Are*. www.TED.com
Duodu, Cameron. "Why are 'witches' still being burned in Ghana?" Dec. 31, 2010, www.guardian.co.uk
Dyer, W. *Pulling Your Own Strings*. New York: Avon Books, 1977.
Dyer, W. *The Sky's the Limit*. New York: Pocket Books, 1980.
Dyer, W. *Your Erroneous Zones*. New York: Avon, 1976.
Engstrand, Beatrice. *The Gift of Healing: A Legacy of Hope*. Wynwood Press,1990.
Frankl, V. *Man's Search for Meaning*. New York: Pocket Books, 1972.
Fuller, G. E. *How to Learn a Foreign Language*. Washington D.C.: Storm King Press, 1987.
Garrison, Marc. *Financially Free*. New York: Simon and Schuster, 1986.
Gentz, W., Roddy, Lee et al. *Writing to Inspire: A Guide to Writing and Publishing for the Expanding Religious Market*. Cincinatti, Ohio: Writer's Digest Books, 1982.
Girard, Joe. *How to Sell Anything to Anybody*. New York: Warner Books, 1977.
Gladwell, Malcolm. *Outliers: the story of success*. Little, Brown & Co., 2008.
Haley, Alex. *The Autobiography of Malcolm X*. New York: Ballantine Books, 1992.
Helmstetter, S. *You can Excel in Times of Change*. New York: Pocket Books, 1991.
Highet, Gilbert. *The Art of Teaching*. New York: Vintage Books, 1950.
Hill, Napoleon. *Grow Rich with Peace of Mind*. New York: Fawcett-Crest, 1967.
Hill, N. & Keown, H. E. *Succeed and Grow Rich through Persuasion*. New York: Fawcett Crest, 1970.
Holmes, E. *The Power of an Idea*. Compiled and edited by Willis Kinnear. Los Angeles, California: Science of Mind Publications, 1965.
Keller, Helen. *The Story of My Life*. Ed. John Albert Macy. NY: Doubleday Page & Co., 1905.

Kiam, V. *Live to Win: Achieving Success in Life and Business.* New York: Harper and Row, 1989.

Kurtzig, Sandra. *CEO: Building a 400 Million Dollar Company from the Ground Up.* Cambridge, Mass.: Harvard Business Press, 1991.

L'Amour, Louis. *Education of a Wandering Man.* New York: Bantam Books, 1989.

Lawrence, R. S. *A Guide To Public Speaking: How To Speak Confidently and Convincingly on Every Kind of Public Occasion.* London: Pan Books, 1963.

Legler, H. *How To Make The Rest of Your Life the Best of Your Life.* New York: Pocket Books, 1970.

Maathai, Wangari. "The Nobel Peace Prize 2004 Wangari Maathai Nobel Lecture." www.nobelprize.org/

Maggio, Rosalie. *The Beacon Book of Quotations by Women.* Boston, Mass.: Beacon Press, 1992.

Mandino, Og. *The Greatest Salesman in the World.* New York: Bantam, 1974.

McCormack, Mark H. *What They Don't Teach You at Harvard Business School: Notes from a Street-Smart Executive.* Bantam Dell Publishing Group, 1984.

New Encyclopaedia Britannica, The. Chicago: Encyclopaedia Britannica Inc. www.britannica.com

Newman, M. & Berkowitz, B. *How to take Charge of Your Life.* New York: Harcourt Brace Jovanovich, 1977.

Peale, Norman Vincent. *Enthusiasm Makes the Difference.* New York: Fawcett Crest, 1967.

Peale, N. V. *The New Art of Living.* Pawling, New York: FCL, 1937.

Peters, Tom. *A Passion for Excellence: The Leadership Difference.* New York: Warner Books, 1986.

Rifenbark, K. R. & Johnson, D. *How to Beat the Salary Trap.* New York: Avon, 1978.

Robbins, Anthony. *Awaken the Giant Within: How to Take Immediate Control of Your Mental, Emotional, Physical and Financial Destiny.* New York: Summit Books, 1994.

Robbins, A. *Unlimited Power.* New York: Fawcett Columbine, 1986.

Sinetar, Marsha. *Developing a 21st Century Mind.* New York: Ballantine Books, 1963.

Spence, Gerry. *How to Argue and Win Every Time: At Home, At Work, In Court, Everywhere, Everyday.* NY: St. Martin's Griffin, 1996.

Stefoff, R. Nelson *Mandela: A Voice Set Free.* New York: Fawcett Columbine, 1990.

"Study Backs Up Strategies for Achieving Goals." www.dominican.edu/

Temko, N. *To Win or To Die.* New York: William Morrow and Company, 1987.

Waitley, Dennis. *Seeds of Greatness.* New York: Pocket Books, 1984.

INDEX

A

Africa, 65, 85, 87, 124, 142, 143, 144
African, 30, 86, 87, 123, 124, 142
African American, 170
African Studies, 123
Alexander the Great, 6
American Business Conference, 107
Antony, Mark, 29
Apartheid, 86
Apollo, 71
April Fool's Day, 119
Ashanti, 91
Ashton, Liz, 122
ASK Computer Systems, 33
Automated Data Processing, 64

B

Bar exam, 38, 39
Begin, Menachem, 89, 90
Bible, 52, 74, 123, 125
Big Brothers/Big Sisters National Hero Award, 107
Bishop University, 149
Black College Fund, 124
Borlaug, Norman E., 172
Branson, Richard, 17, 166, 167, 168, 169
Brisk-de-Lita, 89
Britain, 40
Bryant College, 102
Buber, Martin, 95
Burnaby, British Columbia, 118, 162
Bush, George H., 73

C

Caesar, Julius, 29
Campagnola, Iona, 152
Carnegie, Dale, 7, 35, 57
Carson, Dr. Benjamin, 21, 103
Caruso, Enrico, 56, 57, 58
Charlemagne, 6
Chesterfield, Lord, 116
Children's Museum of the Arts, 107
Christian, 52, 144
Chrysler, 22
Churchill, Sir Winston, 29, 40, 41, 45
Clifford, Clark, 91
Clinton, Bill, 78
Clinton, Hillary, 107
Columbia-Presbyterian Babies Hospital, 128
Congressional Record, 107
Coolidge, Calvin, 38
Copernican theory, 31
Cornell University, 130, 169, 175
Cousins, Norman, 84
Creativity, 50, 101, 118, 130
Csikszentmihalhyi, Mihaly, 18

D

Daving, Dr. Bruce, 128
Degree(s), 6, 7, 32, 83, 85, 123, 130, 144, 172, 175,
Discrimination, 43, 45, 146
Doctorate, 124, 170
Doctor(s), medical, 17, 50

E

Edison, Thomas, 31, 36, 46
Einstein, Albert, 103
Emory University Legend Award, 107
England, 40, 86, 96, 124, 176
Engstrand, Beatrice, 127, 128, 129, 130
Entrepreneur, 7, 8, 19, 32, 33, 108, 109, 110, 111, 134, 135, 154, 159, 160, 166, 168, 169, 174, 178
Erickson, Arthur, 118
Esaw, Johnny, 7, 152
Europe, 40, 62, 65, 160, 163
Everest, Mount, 71, 116

F

Feminine Force, 73, 74
Fijian islands, 32
Filer, Maxcy, 39, 40
Flexible, 42, 47, 65, 106, 112
Florida International University, 164
Ford Motor Company, 47
France, 124, 149, 150

G

Galileo, 31, 36
Gandhi, Mahatma, 6, 31, 36, 42, 43, 45, 56, 87, 99, 178
Gates, Bill, 54, 65, 84, 88, 103, 178
GE Computer Timesharing Service, 32
George Peabody College, 123
Gettysburg, 90
Ghana, 66, 85, 87, 123, 124
Goals,
  - short term, 106
  - medium term, 106
  - long term, 106
God, 22, 53, 77, 81, 82, 83, 100
Goethe, 61, 67
Gore, Tipper, 107
Greek, 32
Guinness Book of World Records, 136

H

Halcyon Communications, 32
Harvard Law School Forum, 85
Harvard University, 56, 85, 133, 144
Helps, Arthur, 138
Henry, Patrick, 103
Hill, Napoleon, 71
Hillary, Sir Edmund, 116
Hollywood, 17
Holmes, Marjorie, 81
Humanities scholar, 130

I

Iacocca, Lee, 22
Ibadan University, 85
Ikeda, Kazuyoshi, 98
India, 6, 31, 42, 141, 174
International Management Group, 132

J

Jacki's Inc., 48
Jackson, Michael, 51, 136
Johnson, Anna, 83
Johnson, Magic, 59
Juilliard School of Music, 20

K

Keller, Helen, 62, 63, 68
Kente, 91
King Jr., Martin Luther, 6, 43, 56, 90, 105, 178
King, Larry, 22
Kipling, Rudyard, 22
Kurtzig, Sandra, 32, 33
Kyushu University, 98

L

L'Amour, Louis, 51, 87, 88, 89, 95
Lewis, Mendi Desalines Shirley, 124
Lewis, Shirley A.R., 123
Lexus, 105
Lillian Vernon Corporation, 107-112, 151
Lincoln, Abraham, 6, 22, 51, 71, 90, 105
Longsthreth, T. Morris, 60
Loreto, Irish Order of, 141
Lowell, Lawrence, 56
Lynn, Loretta, 107

M

Mailer, Norman, 73
Maltz, Maxwell, 70
Mandela, Nelson, 6, 23, 131
MANMAN, 32, 33
Mars, 71
McCormack, Mark H., 132. 133
McCormick, Richard, 28
McDonald's, 60
Mead, Dr. Margaret, 3, 125
Mecca, 85
Medical College of Pennsylvania, 127, 130
Meharry Medical College, 123
Memory, 26, 57, 63, 125
Mercedes, 105
Michelangelo, 21
Microsoft, 84, 87, 178,
Milton, John, 37
Missionaries of Charity, 141
Morita, Akio, 23
Mosbacher, Georgette, 73
Mosbacher, Robert, 73
Muhammad, Elijah, 85

N

Naples, 56
Napoleon, 6, 70
National Taiwan University, 176
Nehru, Jawaharlal, 42
New Encyclopaedia Britannica, The, 40
Newton, Isaac, 107
New York University, 107
Nigeria, 85
Nkrumah, Kwame, 87
Nobel prize, 7, 96, 144
Nutcracker, The, 20

O

Oakland University, 174
Olympics, Special, 48
Owens, Jesse, 21

P

Perkins Institute for the Blind, 62
Personal Power, 75
Plato, 178
Polanyi, John C., 96
Positive Thinking, 6, 77
Proverb, 38
   - African, 30
   - Chinese, 79
Psychiatrist, 77
Psychologist, 47, 69, 76, 77, 125
Public Speaking, 29, 34, 37, 90, 91
Pyrrhic victory, 53

Q

Queen of Busy, 125

R

Radcliffe College, 62
Rhodes scholar, 78
Robbins, Tony, 6, 19, 38
Roddy, Lee, 51
Role model(s), 22, 117, 119, 121
Roosevelt, Eleanor, 36
Roosevelt, Franklin D., 34
Rosenman, Yehuda, 89
Royal Military Academy, 40

S

Sacrifice(s), 138, 139, 145
Schwarzenegger, Arnold, 107
Scouts, Boy, 16
Self-confidence, 72, 73, 77, 78, 80
Self-discipline, 8, 15, 60, 61, 67, 68, 81
Self-esteem, 15, 69, 73, 76, 77
Self-examination, 15
Shakespeare, William, 29, 59
Simon Fraser University, 118
Sinatra, Frank, 107
Smith, Dr. Joseph B., 128
Smith, Eleanor J., 170
Sorensen, Jacki, 48
Spelman College, 124
Spence, Gerry, 83
Stanford University, 55, 117, 123, 124

Stern, Madeleine, 48
Stone, W. Clement, 6
South Africa(n), 6, 17, 86, 98,
Spielberg, Steven, 51, 107
Success, fear of, 30
Sullivan, Anne, 62
Suzuki, David, 151, 161

T

Tchaikovsky, 20
Television, 61, 84, 85, 92, 139, 164, 177
Temko, Ned, 89
Temple University, 134, 175
Tenzing, Sherpa Norgay, 116
Teresa, Mother, 6, 141, 142
Think Big, 21
Third World Press, 124
Thoreau, Henry David, 27, 84
Thurston, Howard, 35
Timbuktu, 17
Trotman, Alex, 47
Truman, Harry, 87
Twain, Mark, 83

U

United Methodist Church, 124
University of California, Berkeley, 124
University of Chicago, 18
University of Pennsylvania, 123, 175
University of Tehran, 163, 164
University of Texas, 122
University of Toronto, 96, 122, 156
University of Washington, 176
University of Wisconsin, Parkside, 170
U.S. West Inc., 28

V

Van Norman Law School, 39
Vernon, Lillian, 107-112
Virginia Beach, 109
Visualization, 22, 102, 104, 105, 114, 115, 130

W

Washington, D.C., 101
Washington Star, 82
Weston, Josh, 64
West Virginia, 123
Wharton School, 107
Whitaker, Larry, 32
White, Betty, 107
Winnipeg Art Gallery, 149
Wolfe, Thomas, 49
Woman's Day, 82
Wright Brothers, 30

X

X, Malcolm, 43, 84, 85, 86

RESOURCES

The following list is meant to provide you with a sampling of the wide range of courses and tools, free or low cost, available on the Internet.

There are many others not mentioned here. Search for whatever you desire; there's a good chance you will find what you want.

If what you are looking for does not exist, remember that there is a name for it: opportunity!

The world awaits your contributions!

- **About**
  www.about.com
  A good starting point for learning about practically any subject. Very good content; useful links.

- **academicearth**
  www.academicearth.org
  A world-class education at your fingertips
  (Yale, Stanford, Carnegie-Mellon, Dartmouth College, etc.)

- **African Virtual University**
  www.avu.or/
  The leading PanAfrican eLearning Network.

- **Alice**
  www.alice.org
  A new way to teach programming (3D).

- **Alison**
  www.alison.com/courses
  Free online courses: accounting, human resources, graphic design, etc..

- **Arduino**
  www.arduino.cc
  Open-source electronic prototyping platform allowing you to create interactive electronic objects.

- **Bartleby**
  www.bartleby.com
  Great Books Online: classics, literature, nonfiction, etc..

- **BBC - Learning**
  (British Broadcasting Corporation)
  www.bbc.co.uk/learning/onlinecourses/
  Foreign languages, computers, math, first aid, sports, etc..

- **Bookboon**
  www.bookboon.com
  Download free books: communication, IT, accounting, marketing, etc..

- **Canadian Virtual University**
  www.cvu-uvc.ca/
  Partnership of Canadian universities offering over 250 courses, diplomas, degrees, through distance learning.

- **Codecademy**
  www.codecademy.com
  Learn how to code and create interactive websites.

- **Confucius Institute Online**
  www.english.chinese.cn
  Learn Chinese free of charge.

- **Cookie**
  www.cookie.com
  Educational games and activities for children

- **Course Hero**
  www.coursehero.com/
  Helping students learn more effectively. College/High school/Students of all ages.

- **Coursera**
  www.coursera.org
  Free online courses Over 30 universities participation.

- **Duolingo**
  www.duolingo.com
  Learn foreign languages for free.

- **EDU - YouTube**
  www.youtube.com/education.

- **edx**
  www.edx.org
  The future of Online Education - for anyone, anywhere, anytime (Harvard, MIT, University of California, Berkeley, etc.).

- **Encyclopedia - Free online**
  www.encyclopedia.com
  Online dictionary and encyclopedia with pictures, facts, and videos.

- **Encyclopedia of Life**
  www.eol.org
  Scientific knowledge on animals and plants.

- **Entrepreneurship Corner (Stanford)**
  www.ecorner.stanford.edu
  Free online archive of podcasts and videos on enterpreneurship, leadership, innovation, etc..

- **Free Chinese**
  www.freechineselessons.com
  Learn to speak, read and write Chinese.

- **Future Learn**
  www.futurelearn.com
  UK based massive open online courses.

- **Google Books**
  www.books.google.com/
  Search and preview millions of books from libraries around the world.

- **Google Scholar**
  www.scholar.google.com/
  Access to information, scholarly literature in a wide variety of fields.

- **Great Books Project**
  www.greatbooks.com
  Resources on some of the best books in the Western literary canon.

- **Great Courses, The**
  www.thegreatcourses.com
  Video lectures by top professors.

- **Hackety Hack!**
  www.hackety.com
  Learn the absolute basics of programming.

- **Harvard Classics, The**
  www.openculture.com
  Free collection of books: history, literature, philosophy, etc..

- **Homeschooling Online**
  www.etap.org/
  Elementary school
  Middle school
  High school

- **Indiegogo**
  www.indiegogo.com
  Fund yourself through indiegogo's platform.

- **ItunesU**
  www.itunesu.com
  Gain access to video and audio lectures from over 800 universities around the world.

- **JSTOR**
  www.jstor.org
  Access to scholarly journals, books, and primary sources.

- **Khan Academy**
  www.khanacademy.org
  Over 3000 videos - arithmetic, physics, finance, history, etc..

- **Kickstarter**
  www.kickstarter.com
  A funding platform for creative projects.

- **Kiva**
  www.kiva.org/start
  Lenders make small loans to borrowers around the world.

- **LearnersTV**
  www.learnerstv.com
  Video lectures: biology, physics, chemistry, mathematics, computer science, medicine, dentistry, etc.

- **LessonPlanet**
  www.lessonplanet.com
  Lesson plans and work sheets for teachers.

- **littleBits**
  www.littlebits.cc/
  Open source library of electronic modules that snap together with magnets for prototyping, learning, and fun.

- **Mechanical MOOC**
  www.mechanicalmooc.org
  Learn Python programming.

- **MIT Open Courseware**
  www.ocw.mit.edu/courses/index.htm
  Free MIT courses: videos, lecture notes, simulations, etc. .

- **Mobento**
  www.mobento.com
  Videolearning platform: Astrobiology/Design/Philosophy to Startups and Technology.

- **Nalanda U**
  Education Unlimited
  www.nalandau.com
  Top quality educational materials in easily accessible form.

- **Nightingale Conant**
  www.nightingale.com
  Personal development resources - books, audio, videos, etc...

- **Norton Literature Online**
  www.norton.com/
  Resources for literature students.

- **Open Culture**
  www.openculture.com
  The best free cultural and educational media on the web. Learn languages/Take free online courses.

- **Pathwright**
  www.pathwright.com
  Launch your own online school with the Pathwright package.

- **Pencil Kings**
  www.pencilkings.com
  Learn how to draw and paint from professional artists.

- **Program on Negotiation,** The (Harvard)
  www.pon.harvard.edu/
  Links to courses on negotiation, articles, books, etc..

- **Project Gutenberg**
  www.gutenberg.org
  Over 30,000 free ebooks.

- **Robomind**
  www.robomind.net
  A simple educational programming language that will familiarize you with the basics of computer programming.

- **Saylor**
  www.saylor.org
  Free online courses - designed by professors.

- **School of Webcraft (Mozilla)**
  https://p2pu.org
  - Peer to Peer University
  - Learn coding
  - Gain recognition for your skills

- **Scratch**
  www.scratch.mit.edu
  A programming language for everyone. Create interactive stories, games, music, art, etc..

- **ShowMe**
  www.showme.com
  Create beautiful tutorials; the easiest way to create and share lessons on the iPad.

- **SpanishMOOC**
  www.spanishmooc.com/
  Learn Spanish and take university courses in Spanish.

- **Stanford Encyclopedia of Philosophy**
  www.plato.stanford.edu
  Access to articles on philosophy and other related topics.

- **Straighterline**
  www.straighterline.com/
  Offers online courses for college credit.

- **SUCCESS Magazine**
  www.successmagazine.com
  Source for inspiration and tips on reaching for your goals.

- **Teachers pay Teachers**
  www.teacherspayteachers.com
  An open marketplace for educators.

- **TED (Technology, Entertainment, & Design)**
  www.ted.com
  Riveting talks by remarkable people, free to the world.

- **TEDED**
  www.ed.ted.com
  Lessons worth sharing.

- **The Virtual Instructor**
  www.thevirtualinstructor.com
  Free Art lessons, Instruction, and Videos.

- **Toastmasters International**
  www.toastmastersinternational.com
  Public speaking club with branches around the world.

- **Top Hat Monocle**
  www.tophatmonocle.com/
  A web-based clicker and online homework tool.

- **2U**
  www.2u.com/
  Quality online programs.

- **Udacity**
  www.udacity.com
  Free courses in computer science, mathematics, etc..

- **Udemy**
  www.udemy.com
  Online courses from the World's Experts.

- **University of the People**
  www.uopeople.org
  Tuition free university dedicated to the democratization of higher education.

- **Wikipedia**
  www.wikipedia.org
  Free encyclopedia collaboratively created with wiki software.

- **Wikiversity**
  http://e.wikiversity.org/
  Devoted to learning resources, learning projects and research from pre-school to professional training and informal learning.

- **World Education University**
  www.theweu.com
  Free online courses.

Author's Note

If you have found this book useful, please tell others about it through your blog, newsletter, article, or other network. Thanks very much.

Everett Ofori, MBA
(Heriot-Watt University, Scotland, UK)

"Speak with passion; live with passion; you'll never be out of fashion."

www.ingramcontent.com/pod-product-compliance
Lightning Source LLC
Chambersburg PA
CBHW051433290426
44109CB00016B/1538